Constructing Meaning
Through Kid-Friendly
Comprehension Strategy Instruction

Nancy N. Boyles

Constructing Meaning Through Kid-Friendly Comprehension Strategy Instruction
©2004 Nancy N. Boyles
All Rights Reserved. Reproducible pages in this resource and on the CD may be
duplicated for classroom-use only.

Dr. Nancy N. Boyles is also the author of *Hands-On Literacy Coaching,
Teaching Written Response to Text, That's a GREAT Answer!*, and *RTI Comprehension Instruction with
Shared Reading: 40 Model Lessons for Intermediate Readers.*

"Myrtle" is from *One World At a Time*, by Ted Kooser, (c) 1985. Reprinted by
permission of the University of Pittsburgh Press.

Book design: She' Heaton
Cover design: Sommer Renaldo

Library of Congress cataloging in publication information:

Boyles, Nancy N., 1948-
   Constructing meaning through kid-friendly comprehension strategy instruction / by
Nancy N. Boyles.
       p. cm.
   Includes bibliographical references.
   ISBN 0-929895-74-6 (pbk.)
   1. Reading comprehension—Study and teaching (Elementary) I. Title.
   LB1573.7.B69 2004
   372.47—dc22

                                                                    2004006369

ISBN-13: 978-0-929895-74-1
ISBN-10: 0-929895-74-6

10 9 8 7 6 5

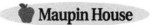

Maupin House Publishing, Inc.
2416 NW 71st Place
Gainesville, FL 32653
800-524-0634
www.maupinhouse.com

Maupin House publishes professional resources K-12 educators. Contact us for tailored, in-school
training or to schedule an author for a workshop or conference. Visit www.maupinhouse.com for
free lesson plan downloads.

To Roberta Naumann Bishop,
Mother, Mentor, Friend—
Thank you for your inspiration and your wisdom,
and for always leading by example.

CONTENTS

Introducing Comprehension Strategies Together for Better Understanding

Embedding Comprehension Strategies During Shared, Guided, and Independent Reading

LIST OF TABLES

**Chapter Seven: Teaching Reading Comprehension Strategies in
                 Shared, Guided, and Independent Reading**

**Chapter Eight: Assessing Students' Reading Comprehension
                 and Comprehension Strategy Use**

INTRODUCTION

A New View
of Comprehension Strategy Instruction

"Teach the reader, not the reading!"

When I said these words during a recent workshop, a school district administrator in the audience asked me to repeat them. So I obliged; "We need to teach the reader, not the reading!"

It's a simple concept. But sometimes we teachers get so wrapped up in teaching the *content* of a text – the characters, the main ideas, and the themes — we forget what should be a critical focus of our instructional mission: helping students *use that text* to understand, not only the content of text, but also to understand and use the comprehension strategies that good readers use automatically to construct meaning from what they read.

If our students are to become good readers, if they are to improve as readers, we must teach them to think about how they think while they read. And that's what I mean by "teach the reader, not the reading!"

Of course, we really do need to teach both the reader *and* the reading. If our reading comprehension lessons don't empower our students to apply comprehension strategies to what they read to more successfully identify and analyze critical elements of the text, plot, characters, and conflict, we've missed our instructional mark.

Teaching the reader is surely the goal of every literacy teacher. Each of us wants to be more effective to help even the most delayed reader to actively engage with the text. At the same time, as teachers, we want to use our hard-earned knowledge about reading, knowledge we have acquired over time. And we want to teach reading comprehension in a balanced, comprehensive literacy program, but without adding a burdensome "something extra" to our already-full curricula.

Are such goals compatible? Yes! You *can* create an interactive, integrated and comprehensive plan to make comprehension strategy instruction a central focus of your balanced literacy program. And in this book, I will show you how!

My Journey from Teacher of Reading to Teacher of Readers

When I first started teaching, in the 1970s, I thought I was a pretty terrific teacher of reading comprehension. In college, I had learned everything there was to know about Bloom's Taxonomy. So, as a teacher, I focused on higher levels of thinking just as I had been taught to do. *After reading,* I would ask my students wonderful questions that probed and plumbed the excellent children's literature I had carefully selected for them. And children in my classroom thought inferentially, critically, and creatively. Well, maybe *some* of them did. But others, I noticed, seemed stymied by even the most literal questions that required them to describe a character or summarize the plot.

I wondered whether I was supporting these challenged readers enough *before* reading. So I tried to activate their prior knowledge. This approach helped my struggling readers, especially, to make predictions and set a purpose before they engaged the text. Still, when I looked around my classroom, I didn't sense that I had yet helped my most challenged readers enough.

The "good readers" were fine. They were focused, and they moved seamlessly from one literacy activity to another with a good deal of independence. But, despite my best efforts, many of the struggling readers in my classes still spent precious little time in their seats reading. Instead, they fidgeted, sent themselves on urgent missions to various destinations or looked longingly through the window at the playground. I could see that reading wasn't among their favorite things to do. It wasn't anything that absorbed their attention the way reading can fascinate a good reader.

During small-group, guided reading sessions, these struggling readers would often abruptly stop and look pleadingly in my direction when they encountered a word they didn't recognize. I knew I could help them sound out the words. But even when they got the words right, I noticed how seldom they understood the meaning of what they read. My simple questions to these students often elicited only blank stares. And I rarely attempted to push them to interpret or evaluate a text. I felt that these children needed assistance *during the reading process itself.* But how do you help kids *while* they read?

I suspect that many teachers can relate to these classroom experiences. We all want our instruction to be effective for every child in the classroom. We want to encourage and support our students as we lead them to reading independence. But, for me, it was not until I applied the explicit teaching model to my reading comprehension instruction that I began to feel that my worthy goals as a teacher had become reality for the majority of my students.

By 1998, I was no longer working full-time as a classroom teacher, but had joined the faculty of the School of Education at Southern Connecticut State University. And I had begun to read research that described the benefits of teaching comprehension strategies explicitly. (See pages 250–253 "Bibliography of Professional Resources" to access the research evidence that guided my work with comprehension strategies.) I had always been a fan of explicit teaching. The success of this instructional model is due to a gradual, systematic release of responsibility for learning, from teacher to student. The process begins with the teacher explaining and modeling the new task, followed by ample opportunities for students to practice and then reflect on what they've learned. This systematic approach is repeated with increasing levels of independence until students master the new task. The more I learned about this teaching model, the more I wondered how it might apply to the teaching of comprehension strategies. I began to imagine the possibilities.

During this time, due to my concurrent work as a literacy consultant, I still visited elementary school classrooms in many different school districts. And it was on one such visit, to a fifth-grade, urban classroom, which had more than its share of challenges, when a new instructional door opened for me, and I stepped through it. As my reading lesson progressed that day, I noticed that I was teaching reading comprehension strategies in a way that supported my students while they were reading! As they learned about strategies, the kids began talking about literature deeply and passionately! The explicit teaching model had altered fundamentally the traditional dynamics of interaction between teacher,

I noticed I was teaching reading strategies in a way that supported my students while they were reading!

students, and text. And I became convinced that day of the value of the explicit teaching model for reading comprehension.

Moving beyond Conventional Wisdom

For me, explicit teaching opened the door of learning wide enough to allow a new perspective on how to teach reading comprehension strategies. And since my first "trial run" with this teaching method in 1998, I've had the opportunity to share my experiences with this method with many teachers and students.

I always begin by asking teachers to think about comprehension strategy instruction a little differently than they may have thought about it before. Popular books about comprehension strategy instruction typically recommend teaching one broadly defined strategy at a time over an extended period, several weeks, to proficiency, before moving on to teach the next comprehension strategy. No book, at least that I've found, has addressed the benefits to students when teachers move beyond teaching the individual strategies to show their students how to blend the strategies together while they read.

But why not? After all, "real readers" don't read by isolating a single strategy. We don't use just one strategy while reading to construct meaning from everything we read for six or seven weeks. I wouldn't think to myself, "I'll just make connections for the next several weeks when I read the newspaper." Or, "Just for fun, I'll just visualize when I read the next couple of novels, but won't use any other strategies to understand the text." Of course not!

Instead, competent readers have a repertoire of reading strategies available, strategies that we mix and match *while* we read. Competent readers automatically know when to ask a question instead of make a connection. And each of us applies these strategies as needed, as we are reading, depending on our personal learning style and the demands of the text.

I wanted to find a way to teach reading comprehension to children in a way that would help them to competently use various reading strategies, of course. But I also wanted to help children to use those strategies flexibly, to best suit their needs and the demands of the text before them.

The traditional approach of teaching one strategy over a long period of time implies that learning reading comprehension strategies is difficult and students need many weeks to master even one of these strategies. But my experiences have shown me that students can grasp the basics of several comprehension strategies quite easily. It's the fine points of the strategies that take time for them to learn. Mastery is a long-term goal and doesn't need to occur all at once.

However, strategy instruction that I've observed in classrooms makes no clear distinction between *introducing* the strategies and *refining* them. Most of the comprehension-strategy instruction I've witnessed targets the modeling and practicing of one, broadly defined reading comprehension strategy, over and over again until students get good at it. Teachers talk about "inferring" or "visualizing" or "questioning." It's a little like saying to a student, "Today we are going to learn about subtraction." The broad concept is just too big for students to "get" in a lesson or even a series of lessons.

It makes more sense to introduce students to a manageable repertoire of strategies initially. Then, as they practice using several, blended strategies, the teacher can see which strategies students are applying well and which strategies are more difficult for students. In this way, comprehension strategy teaching can become more focused. Rather than teaching an intensive lesson on a broadly defined strategy — connecting or visualizing, for example — you can zero-in on a *specific application* of a strategy to the study of literature or informational text.

You might tell your students, "Today, let's work on connecting to characters," or, "Let's see if we can visualize our new vocabulary in the next social studies chapter." This more focused approach encourages the teacher to spend a few days on a particular application of a strategy through shared, guided, and independent reading, then move on to another application of the same strategy or a different strategy. Over time, the teacher can return to each strategy on many occasions, but teach it with a different application each time.

We know what happens when we teach something intensively and then fail to return to it for months: students lose what they don't use. All of the learning about a particular strategy doesn't need to (and, in fact, probably shouldn't) occur at once. Students need to have their learning reinforced on a regular, consistent basis to retain what they have been taught. Keeping *all* the reading comprehension strategies "front and center" helps students remember the purposes of these strategies and how to use them as they are reading.

Additionally, when we go the route of teaching one strategy at a time, our emphasis too easily becomes "getting good at the strategy," rather than getting good at reading comprehension. But when we teach kids to apply these reading comprehension strategies as a package, we are more likely to remain focused on our real goal, empowering children to understand what they read.

Helping students to understand what they read should be the central focus of any comprehensive literacy program. But teaching reading comprehension strategies need not be something you "add on" to your "regular" curriculum. As you will learn in the chapters of this book, teaching these strategies can be and should be an important part of what happens every day in your classroom during shared, guided and independent reading, whether your students are reading fiction or nonfiction.

How this Book Empowers Teachers

As a result of my consistently positive experiences using the explicit teaching instructional model to teach reading comprehension strategies, I am convinced that this instructional model is no educational fad; it's not a gimmick. (And in 2001, explicit teaching became a national educational priority as the instructional model mandated in the No Child Left Behind legislation passed by Congress and signed into law by the President that year.)

The ways I apply the instructional model in this book to teaching reading comprehension strategies can benefit just about any student operating at a reasonable level of reading fluency (second grade or above). This book will show you how to 1) introduce your students quickly to a range of comprehension strategies 2) model your own uses of comprehension strategies while you read out loud to your students 3) give your students ample opportunity for practice using these strategies and 4) refine their use of comprehension strategies through specific strategy applications.

The model I provide in this book is intended to be part of the developmental literacy curriculum although it would also be useful as an intervention strategy. This model can be especially helpful for transitional readers who are making the leap from "easy reader" books to early chapter books and more advanced children's literature. This model also works well with delayed readers in middle school or high school. And younger children in kindergarten and first grade – as well as older students who are still reading on a primary level — can access reading comprehension strategies taught explicitly through read-alouds and shared reading if the teacher uses quality text that invites student reflection and response.

Throughout this book, you'll find lesson plans and charts to, first, help you get started and, next, support your strategy instruction using the explicit teaching model. These materials, which are all copyrighted, are available in this book for your use, both in paper format for photocopying to suit your needs and also as Microsoft Word files on the CD in the envelope inside the back cover this book. The electronic files, especially, will allow you to easily customize the reproducibles to meet your classroom needs.

Introducing Comprehension Strategies Together for Better Understanding will introduce you to the explicit teaching model as I have applied it to teaching the entire range of comprehension strategies. In Chapter One, I show you how to give your students a quick, kid-friendly introduction to several reading comprehension strategies so they can begin to practice using these strategies as an integrated whole while they are reading. You will learn in this chapter to introduce a manageable repertoire of reading comprehension strategies, rather than initiate a long study of one strategy.

Chapter Two shows how to model, during Read-Aloud/Think-Aloud sessions with your whole class, the ways you, the experienced reader, use comprehension strategies to understand what you read. Next, Chapter Three will show you how to offer your students the opportunities they need to practice using comprehension strategies in teacher-guided small groups. Chapter Four will help you move your reading comprehension instruction past good to great by targeting individual strategy applications.

Embedding Reading Comprehension Strategies during Shared, Guided, and Independent Reading includes instructional tools for refining students' uses of comprehension strategies, including a plan to keep reading comprehension strategies "front and center" throughout all parts of your balanced literacy program. Also in this section of the book

Throughout this book, you'll find lesson plans and charts to help you get started and support your strategy instruction.

are several suggestions and tools for assessing how well your students understand and apply each strategy and all the strategies together.

Chapter Five shows you how to apply your strategy instruction to the study of fiction. In Chapter Six you will discover how your instruction in the content areas, such as science or social studies, offers valuable opportunities for your students to apply reading comprehension strategies to nonfiction, including textbooks. In Chapter Seven, you will learn to embed comprehension strategy instruction in shared, guided and independent reading.

To help you assess your students' use of the entire repertoire of comprehension strategies, Chapter Eight offers helpful ideas and tools for assessing, both orally and through written assignments, your students' abilities to apply comprehension strategies to what they read. And this chapter shows you how to assess the most important measure of your reading comprehension instruction, how well your students understand what they read as a result of their use of these strategies. (While the assessment tools provided in Chapter Eight include some written assessments, the teaching model presented in this book does not address in specific the craft of responding in writing to text-based comprehension questions. Of course, responding to reading in writing should be incorporated into any comprehensive literacy model. But for more on that topic, I direct you to my book, *Teaching Written Response to Text,* Maupin House, 2002.)

Strategy Follow-Up Activities includes hands-on resources and bibliographies to help teachers bring meaningful comprehension strategy instruction immediately into their classrooms. These resources include an array of reproducible activity sheets to support instruction.

Annotated Bibliographies of Children's Literature is an extensive bibliography of excellent children's literature selections, and

Strategy Mini-Posters, Cue-Cards and Book Marks offers a range of valuable instructional aids.

Growing Professionally through the Study of Comprehension offers teachers questions useful for professional study-group work. Also included in this section is an extensive bibliography of professional resources that will help you dig deeper as a learner into the topic of reading comprehension.

Throughout this book, you will find the factual information, proven methods, visual aids, and planning templates that will help you bring comprehension strategy instruction to the center of your balanced literacy program. And you will find my heartfelt excitement about the power and potential of this teaching model to improve your students' reading comprehension. My hope is that this book will inspire you even as it informs and empowers you to teach readers about reading.

Introducing Comprehension Strategies Together for Better Understanding

1

Helping Children Think about Thinking: Introducing Reading Comprehension Strategies Using Kid-Friendly Language

- Successful readers use a repertoire of comprehension strategies, not just one at a time.

- Students begin to read more effectively as teachers give them access to a manageable array of reading comprehension strategies.

- Students can start immediately to use and combine these tools *while they read*.

Getting Started

Taking that first step is often the most difficult part of trying anything new in the classroom. And getting started can be the hardest part of teaching reading comprehension, too. We imagine that if we persuasively *introduce* reading comprehension strategies to our students, instruction in these strategies over the next few months will just fall into place. That's probably a bit of wishful thinking, but first impressions can be strong and lasting.

Take heart. Introducing comprehension strategies to your students can be quick, easy, and fun. Keep your explanation simple and offer your students a reasonable portion of new knowledge that satisfies, but does not overwhelm them. Speak in language they can understand, and explain each strategy in a way that is simple enough for *all* the children in your class to succeed. A child's mind can easily become overloaded. So remember; there's always tomorrow or next week to continue the conversation. Our goal for any instruction is to make *today* successful.

You will begin by introducing your students to several strategies with a brief "hands-on, minds-on" explanation that uses terms easy for children to understand. In such an introductory session, which I outline, step-by-step, below, the instructional goal is to explain to students what a reading comprehension strategy is and then identify and introduce several strategies. Mastery of these strategies is not the instructional goal now. The goal is to begin to build a common strategy vocabulary and to establish a foundation for the strategy work ahead. So, rather than drilling students extensively in use of any particular comprehension strategy, you will, instead, in this initial lesson, briefly identify a few strategies and then explain for the students why good readers use these strategies.

Use Visual Aids

Before you begin, prepare some materials. You may want to use the two sets of mini-posters provided on pages 226 - 237 of this book. (These mini-posters are also available in files on the CD inside the back cover. The files for the mini-posters are titled "OneA1" and "OneA2.") I recommend laminating the mini-posters before you use them.

In the first set of mini-posters, the name of one strategy is printed on each poster along with a small picture icon and several bulleted highlights, which state the strategy's main points. These mini-posters with bulleted text work best with grades three and up; the brief definitions help children in these grades to use each strategy accurately right from the start.

In the second set of mini-posters each mini-poster features only the strategy name and a large picture icon, but no bulleted text definitions. This set of mini-posters is ideal for use with the early primary grades and also for ESL students or other youngsters with limited reading skills.

Throughout my introduction, I use mini-posters as a visual aid and a means to involve the children in the lesson. The mini-posters are also used in an interactive exercise at the conclusion of this lesson. Later, I hang the mini-posters prominently in the classroom where students can easily refer to them as they continue learning about comprehension strategies and as they use these strategies in their own reading.

Teach kids to apply these reading comprehension strategies as a package.

Open the Lesson with a Dialogue

I begin by saying to the class, "Suppose I told you that I knew some fourth graders (or students in any grade) who were awesome readers. . . . What do *you* think makes a kid a great reader?"

This is a good opener. With the answers I receive, I learn very quickly whether the students have any background in reading comprehension strategies and what, in their opinions, comprises skilled reading.
"Great readers are excellent at sounding out words."
"Great readers find chunks they know."
"Great readers go back and reread."
"Great readers get their mouth ready."

Most of the responses I hear are "good reader" strategies, acquired for the most part from immersion in primary-level, guided reading instruction. But I've found that even in the intermediate grades, the strategies mentioned generally center on "breaking the code," getting the words right.

I want students to see that great reading goes beyond getting the words right. I want them to recognize that it's not about just "getting your mouth ready," but also about getting your *mind* ready. So I tell them, "Great readers think about their thinking while they read."

For these children (and for most adults, too), "thinking about thinking" will be a new idea. Because the concept of "thinking about thinking" is the basis of the reading comprehension strategies I am about to introduce to them, I spend a few moments to discuss this new – and very important — idea. I want the kids to learn not just *what* each strategy is, but also *why* good readers use thinking strategies to read successfully. I try to make the discussion as interactive as possible.

From Reading to Football and Back Again

"What do I mean by the word *strategy*?" I will ask the class. And sometimes I get a pretty good definition. But other times, it's blank stares. In that case, I will mention football although this is uncertain turf for me. I know almost nothing about this sport, but I proceed anyway.

"Let's talk about football!" I say.
"What are those football guys doing when they're in that huddle?" I ask the kids.

Hands wave excitedly; they usually know the answer to this one! "They're making a plan," the children tell me. "They're figuring out their strategy."

"Why?" I persist. "Why do football players want a strategy?"

"So they can win!" the kids say.

"That's right!" I answer. "They want to win! And it's the same with reading. Good readers use strategies. Good readers think about the strategies they use to win at reading, to really understand what they read. And when you know the right reading strategies to use, you can come up with a winning plan for reading!"

Metacognition: An Important Word

I then introduce the children to the big word we use when we talk about strategies for winning at reading. I hold up the laminated mini-poster that reads, "Metacognition Means Thinking about Thinking." (A paper version of this mini-poster is found on p. 238. And this poster is also on the CD in the file titled, "OneB.") I challenge the class to try to pronounce this big word, *met-a-cog-ni-tion*. Usually someone will come close to getting it right.

Although I generally use easier words when I'm teaching children, I make an exception in this case because there is just no other word that means "thinking about thinking." And my first goal when I initiate comprehension-strategy instruction is to show my students that they can, in fact, think about the way they think. I tell them that we will begin today, right now, to learn the best strategies to use for thinking while we are reading.

Introducing the Strategies

When I'm conducting this initial explanation of metacognitive strategies, I feel a bit like the Energizer Bunny. The kids probably wonder how an otherwise normal-looking adult can get quite so charged up over a bunch of mini-posters. But I keep the pace quick and the level of energy high because I want the children to catch my enthusiasm. Although I'm doing most of the talking, I find ways to invite their participation. And after each strategy has been discussed, I ask one child to come to the front of the room to be "keeper of the poster."

I am careful to teach reading comprehension strategies in language that elementary and middle school students can understand. For this reason, I've changed some of the strategy names that teachers may know best to words that are likely to be within a child's meaning vocabulary. These kid-friendly labels may not be as precise as the more sophisticated terms we see in other books about comprehension strategy instruction, but these words are a fine place for students to begin.

Getting good at using metacognitive strategies can engage teachers and students for a long while; there will be plenty of time down the road for using technical terminology if needed. Here's how the labels I use to introduce reading strategies to children compare to the more technical terms with which teachers may already be familiar:

Comparative Labels
for Explaining Metacognitive Strategies

Technical label	Kid-friendly label
Connecting	Connecting
Using sensory images	Picturing
Questioning	Wondering
Determining importance	Noticing the important parts
Synthesizing	Figuring out
Inferring	Figuring out
Monitoring	Noticing when you stop understanding
A part of Inferring	Predicting/Guessing

Our goal is for students to blend these comprehension strategies comfortably and flexibly as they read. But I briefly define each strategy, one at a time, so students get a clear understanding of what each term means. I also want them to begin thinking about how each strategy contributes to their comprehension of any text they read.

Explaining *Connecting*

Whichever set of mini-posters you are using, whether those that feature the large picture icon or those with the bulleted textual definitions, show the children the mini-poster on *Connecting*.

If students are already aware of any of the reading comprehension strategies, connecting is likely to be the one they will know best, perhaps because when teachers engage in the one-strategy-at-a-time approach, they generally begin with connecting. (And sometimes they seem to remain *stuck* here, too.)

Children need to know that good readers make a lot of different mental connections as they are reading; they connect what they are reading to their background knowledge, to their own life, to another text, and to the larger world. I talk with students about *why* good readers should think about such connections as they are reading.

"Suppose you pick up a book, and as you begin to read it, it just doesn't 'grab' you," I say to my students. "The book doesn't seem to connect to you, to your life in any way. What would you want to do with that book?"

"I would want to put that book back and get another one," is the typical response.

"Yes," I continue. "Good readers do that all the time. We can each think of a time when we haven't wanted to continue reading a certain book, so we placed it back on the shelf and chose a different one. But if we're putting back *every* book we pick up, that's not such a good thing."

(As teachers, we can each likely recall students we've had over the years who beat a constant path back and forth from the library corner in the classroom because they couldn't settle on *any* book.)

"If we try really hard to think of ways a story connects to us and our lives," I continue, "we're more likely to stick with the story. That's one reason it's so important to look for connections. Making connections with the text will help us to keep reading it."

I will then ask someone in the class to come up and hold our *Connecting* mini-poster for everyone to see.

Explaining *Picturing*
"How do the pictures in our mind help us as readers?"

I ask this question as I hold up the *Picturing* mini-poster. The mini-poster version with bulleted text describes the "pictures" we can make in our minds using all five of our senses.

"It's simple," I tell my students. "Pictures help us remember what we've read."

Our goal for any instruction is to make today successful.

To help students (and teachers) understand the value of using the picturing strategy while reading, I ask them to remember a time when they received big news, whether it was good news or bad news.

"Where were you when you got the news?" I ask. "What was the weather like at the time? Who was with you?

"Chances are, you can answer all of these questions. The content of that message, the big news you received, is forever embedded in the context in which you received the news, a context that is made of many different sensory impressions, sights, sounds, scents, tastes, and touch.

"And that's the way it is with reading, too," I tell the students. "When a reader can picture the words on the page as if they were a movie playing, or as if they were actually in the story, themselves, they can more easily remember the words, the message, and replay them again and again. When your reading includes special sensory effects — sights, sounds, scents, tastes, textures — you've got in your own imagination a feature film that rivals any Disney spectacular!"

To explain *picturing* clearly and simply for your students, choose mental images to which children can easily relate. You might ask them to tell what images, sounds, textures, tastes or scents they think of when they read about a pumpkin pie baking in an oven, or a terrible thunderstorm late at night, a fluffy pillow or a yapping puppy. Ask them to think about which sensory details, which mental pictures, bring these ideas to life for them.

When I introduce children to the *picturing* strategy, I want them to understand that the pictures we have in our mind help us respond to text at an emotional level. When we laugh out loud as we read, or when we wipe a tear from our eye over something we've read, it's probably because we can *picture* the scene described in the text. The pictures we have in our mind as we are reading help us to remember the words we read, and they also help us to respond emotionally to the author's message.

When I've completed my brief introduction to *picturing*, I then ask one of the children to come to the front to hold up the *Picturing* mini-poster for everyone to see.

Then we move on to the next strategy.

Explaining *Wondering*

Talk briefly with your students about some of the things good readers might wonder about as they read, such as what might happen next in the story or how the story might end. Then encourage your students to think about why *wondering* is so important to successful reading.

To help students appreciate the value of the wondering strategy, I travel back in time to my own childhood. "When I was a little girl," I tell them, "I used to love to read in bed each night before going to sleep. After a few minutes of this, my mom would holler upstairs, 'Time to turn off your light now!' And I would always answer, 'But I can't go to sleep yet! I just *have* to find out what happens in the next chapter!'"

What does *wondering* do for us as readers? For one thing, it keeps us reading! If we can't wait to find out what happens on the *next* page, the *next* chapter, or by the end of the book, we're going to stick with that book until our questions are answered.

The reading comprehension strategy of *wondering* is more complex than this brief introductory explanation implies. But with *wondering,* as with all the reading comprehension strategies you introduce, children can and will learn much more about the strategy as they get comfortable using it while they read. They can then begin to explore the complexities and the fun of these strategies.

When I've completed my brief introduction to *wondering*, I ask one of the children to come to the front to hold up the *Wondering* mini-poster for everyone to see.

Explaining *Guessing* or *Predicting*

I try to help my students experience for themselves how the reading strategy of *guessing*, which I sometimes also refer to as *predicting*, naturally follows *wondering*.

So I may begin by telling them, "Soon after we have wondered about something we read, we are likely to begin to ponder possible outcomes. We may ask ourselves questions like this: 'Why did that character behave in this way?' Or 'Why did the author include this small detail?' Hmmm. . . We think a while, and then we venture a guess. And maybe our guess is right!

"But when we've made a prediction, a guess about what will happen next in the story, we naturally want to read further, and we want to read carefully, too, to find out if our guess was right — or wrong. That's why guessing is so important," I tell my students, "because once we've made a good guess, we tune in to the text extra carefully to find out if our thinking was on target."

Many metacognitive strategy lists don't specify *guessing/predicting* as an individual strategy, but, instead, include this strategy as a component of *inferring*. However, making predictions about text is so important to good comprehension that I want my students to be able to identify this strategy. So I give it a label they can use, and I use the term, *guessing*, rather than *predicting*, with younger children.

Predicting (or *guessing*) sets the stage for students to monitor their own understanding of text. Formulating reasonable guesses, predictions, from page to page, and then checking to see whether these guesses and predictions are correct is a process that helps a reader to notice when his or her thinking about the text is on-track and when it is off-track.

It's also important for children to begin to use the strategy of *guessing* (*predicting*) because this strategy is also closely related to the next reading comprehension strategy, *noticing*.

When I've completed my brief introduction to the *guessing (predicting)* strategy, I ask another of the children to come to the front to hold up the corresponding mini-poster for everyone to see.

Explaining *Noticing*

I begin introducing this strategy by asking my students, "What are some of the things good readers *notice* as they read?"

When I ask this question, children's immediate response is typically, "They notice the pictures!"

Fair enough. But as teachers, we want kids to realize that good *noticing* also means keying-in to important verbal clues: words, sentences, and paragraphs that offer evidence of the text's meaning. So I tell my students that some of the best clues in stories might be the names of characters, phrases that identify the problem, or sentences that specify important events. And helpful clues for a reader to notice in informational, nonfiction could be the words in bold print or the words that lead us to the main ideas.

But simply collecting these clues isn't enough. So I ask my students, "What do we do with these clues?" They need to recognize that when we find clues in text, we should file them away carefully in our mind so we can pull them out later to see how they all fit together — as main ideas and themes.

I also want my students to know that good readers also *notice* when they stop understanding what they are reading, when none of the clues they've gathered while reading seem to make sense.

"Why is it important to *notice* when you stop understanding?" I will ask my students.

Children often have the right answer to this question; "So you can fix your problem," they may say.

But they're only partly correct about *how* this "fixing" happens. "Sound out the word," they sometimes offer. Or they say, "Read to the end of the sentence." Or, "Read the sentence again."

I want students to *notice* the role of their reading comprehension strategies in addition to their re-reading and using word-level strategies to untangle text. Any and all of these strategies can help a struggling reader to get their comprehension back on track.

When I've completed my brief introduction to the *Noticing* strategy, I ask another child to come to the front to hold up the *Noticing* mini-poster for everyone to see.

Explaining *Figuring Out*

Figuring out is my simplified version of two metacognitive strategies, *synthesis* and *inference*. These are awfully abstract ideas for students in elementary school to understand. (And there are many *teachers* who have difficulty with these concepts, too!) But the concepts are within the grasp of young readers if we make the language we use to discuss these reading strategies meaningful for young readers. And we must do this because *figuring out* is critical to reading.

This process helps a reader to notice when his thinking about the text is on track and when it is off track.

Figuring out moves a student's thinking beyond the construction of basic meaning to a deeper understanding of text. *Figuring out* is also a reading strategy that earns students high scores on state achievement tests. But many comprehension texts overlook the urgency of teaching *figuring out*. The chapter on *synthesis* is often relegated to the very end of these books. And with seven or eight weeks typically devoted to teaching each strategy, *figuring out* is often left out, year after year. But do we really want to allow several years to go by without teaching students how to *synthesize* – to *figure out* – what they are reading? No! Making this abstract strategy accessible to younger children is imperative! And it's doable!

We could spend a lot of valuable classroom time hammering away at definitions of *inference* and *synthesis,* and some of our students would understand. Or we could translate these words to a term that children use every day: *figuring out.*

"Readers figure out different kinds of things as they read," I tell my students, holding up the "figuring out" mini-poster with the funny light bulb on it. "Sometimes," I say, "*figuring out* is like filling in the blanks. For example, the author might write that a certain character calls people names and teases kids who are younger, and this character picks fights, too. The author wants us to *figure out* that this kid is a …. How would you fill in that blank?" I ask my students.

"Bully!" everyone choruses. "He's a bully!"

I then move on to describe a kind of *figuring out* that is more of a *synthesis*. I tell students, "Sometimes when I read, I'm reading along, turning the pages, and all of a sudden, it just hits me; 'I get it!' I say to myself. All of a sudden, I know who committed the crime! I see how all the clues I've been collecting fit together! I understand what the author is trying to tell me! I have *figured out* the meaning! I love when this happens because I feel successful!"

I tell my students, "When you can really *figure out (synthesize)* the meaning of a text, you have used all of your reading comprehension strategies very well. You have made the appropriate connections, created some great pictures in your mind, wondered, guessed, and noticed a lot of clues all along while you were reading. And all of this information has helped you to *figure out* the author's meaning."

There's much more to say about *inferring* and *synthesizing*. But this is enough of an explanation for now. The goal of an initial strategy explanation is not mastery; the goal is simply to begin a conversation that will continue for a very long time. When I've completed my brief introduction to *figuring out*, I ask another child to come to the front to hold up the *Figuring out* mini-poster for everyone to see.

Varying Strategy Introductions

Quickly introducing the complete repertoire of six reading comprehension strategies works well with students in grades three and up. But for younger students, or for struggling readers in grades four and up, or when teaching children whose first language is not English, I begin by explaining just a couple of these strategies. Two strategies are not too many to present to these children at one time. And introducing more than one strategy will offer these students some flexibility in processing text. Maybe a child can't think of any connection to a particular story, but if he or she can get great mental pictures from the text, that will help them to understand what they are reading.

After introducing two strategies, I will then add two more strategies in the next session and then two more until I've introduced the entire set. (See Chapter Four for a sample ten-week schedule for getting started with comprehension strategy instruction, whether for average, intermediate-grade students or for students who are younger or need more support.)

Concluding Your Introduction to Reading Strategies

At the conclusion of your introduction, depending on how many strategies you introduced to your students in this first session, up to six children will be standing before your class, each child holding a mini-poster representing one of the reading strategies you've just introduced.

I like to conclude our strategy-introduction session with a guessing game. The poster-holding children place their poster behind their back so the class can't see the posters.

Then I ask the class, "Can anyone remember one of the strategies we learned about today?"

Even young children do not find it difficult to recall the names of the strategies. And once a student has named one of the strategies, the child holding the poster representing that strategy will display it again for the entire class to see.

I will then ask the class to name another strategy until all of the reading-strategy mini-posters are again held high in front of the class.

Taking Steps Toward Independent Comprehension
We've now introduced the repertoire of strategies in about ten or fifteen minutes and have completed the first leg of our journey toward independent comprehension. At this point, the teacher is still very much in charge of the task-at-hand. But that will change as more and more responsibility for learning is gradually transferred to students. Although independence may seem a long way off at the outset, this goal should be made clear to students right from the start.

"Why do you suppose I'm explaining these strategies to you?" I ask students even in this very first session.

"So we can use them!" kids are quick to respond.

"You're half right," I tell them. "I'm teaching you about these comprehension strategies so you can use them *all by yourselves*, without any assistance from me. I'll give you all the guidance you need so you can get good at these strategies. But each day, you should feel like you can use strategies a little better on your own until one day you realize: wow, I don't need my teacher anymore; I can do this all by myself."

All learners—kids and adults—learn through a similar progression of steps as they master the performance of something new. The explanation of this process described below is based on the Pearson and Gallagher "Gradual Release of Responsibility" model of instruction. (See *Bibliography of Professional Resources*, page 250, for more about this model.) Even young children can comprehend how this instructional model works if it's explained in simple language that they can understand.

My explanation of the *Gradual Release of Responsibility* goes something like this:
*"When I first introduce something new to you, that's a time when **I do, and you watch**. I might be standing in front of the room, or maybe we're all sitting together in the meeting area. First, I explain the new concept (like strategies) to you. I try to keep my explanation short, but I need to say enough so you can understand what I'm doing when I model, or show you,*

how strategy-thinking works. This part takes me about five minutes.

*"The next part of the lesson takes a bit longer, about 15-20 minutes. As I model the new concept, you get a clearer idea of how it works. Gradually, you begin to take on some of the responsibility yourselves. We're still practicing as a whole group, but you start to raise your hand and want to share your good ideas about how you're applying the new learning. That's when **I do, and you help**. If you're not sure about how to do something, this is a perfect time to ask questions, because the next step will be to practice the new learning more on your own.*

*"At that point, **you do, and I help**. Now the 'lesson' is over and you're probably back at your own desk, or maybe you're working with me and a few other students at the reading table. I might look over your shoulder to see how you're doing as you're using strategies with your "just right" book. Or I might give you a couple of suggestions as you share your strategy-thinking out loud when we're reading together in a small group. But mostly, I expect you to do the work without too much help from me. You'll most likely need to practice quite a bit before you get really good at the new learning (strategy-thinking) before we can move on to learn something else new about comprehension strategies. This guided practice could take a few weeks. Getting really good at something takes effort and patience. But when you see how well you're doing, you'll realize that all that practice paid off and you'll feel brilliant!*

*"Eventually, you'll get to the point where **you do, and I watch.** That's independence. When you get to independence with comprehension strategies, you're ready to use the strategies without any help from me. Now <u>you're</u> in charge of the learning. That's totally different from the way we began when I was the one who was in charge."*

When I'm showing this gradual release model to teachers, I demonstrate the reciprocal nature of teacher/learner roles through a diagram:

Explain/Model ⟶ I do, you watch
Structured Practice ⟶ I do, you help
Guided Practice ⟶ You do, I help
Independence ⟶ You do, I watch

Let's move on to the next step here: modeling the strategies to see how modeling can take children another step closer to independence as they pursue excellence in reading comprehension.

Even young children do not find it difficult to recall the names of the strategies.

2

Thinking Out Loud:
Modeling Reading Comprehension Strategies

⚙ Teacher modeling of a new strategy is critical to students' ultimate success with that strategy.

⚙ To help students learn to use reading comprehension strategies well, model your integrated use of multiple strategies; read short texts aloud to your entire class, pausing from time to time to describe the several strategies you are using to understand the text while you read.

⚙ Once your students have had sufficient opportunity to observe you modeling blended-strategy thinking as you read, allow them to share with the class how they are using comprehension strategies to understand the text you are reading.

**Model Comprehension Strategies
in a Whole Class Read-Aloud/Think-Aloud**

As classroom teachers, we often wonder which learning goals are best achieved through instruction that is directed at the whole class, which learning objectives are best accomplished in small-group instruction, and which learning activities students can productively undertake independently. Modeling reading comprehension strategies is an activity that works well with the entire class, as students listen to what the teacher says about comprehension strategies she is using to understand a text.

As you can imagine, modeling strategic thinking during oral reading changes the entire read-aloud experience. For one thing, it takes a teacher much longer to read even a short selection of text when she is describing for her class the thinking strategies she is using to understand the text. The discussion of comprehension strategies breaks the flow of the narrative, whether the text is fiction or nonfiction. And this interruption can, at least initially, even obscure the content of the text. Hence, we need to choose our "think-aloud texts" carefully.

We would, of course, never want to read every text to our students while modeling reading comprehension strategies. But teacher modeling of these strategies is essential if we want our students to begin to use these strategies well on their own while they are reading.

Take Time to Think Out Loud

Because teacher modeling of a new strategy is critical to students' ultimate success using that strategy, teachers must take time to demonstrate for their students in Read-Aloud/Think-Aloud sessions how good readers use comprehension strategies to construct meaning from text. Too many teachers rush through the modeling stage of instruction to get books and pencils into students' hands. Then, when students' individual performance with reading comprehension strategies falls short of teacher expectations, we regret our hurry-up, get-the-show-on-the-road approach.

I sometimes wonder if teacher modeling of reading comprehension strategies is treated superficially because it may seem to the teacher that he or she is doing all the work, not the kids. But these sessions are not intended to be a spectator sport for students. Rather than just "sitting there," however politely, throughout your strategy-modeling session, students should listen actively, noting places in the text where you have used strategies.

A reasonable length of time for most students to remain actively engaged in this type of teacher-modeling session is about 20 minutes. Pause in your oral reading as often as seems needed to describe for your students the comprehension strategies you are using to understand the text. Read one small chunk of the text and pause to describe the comprehension strategy you are using. Then read the next chunk. Continue in this process of reading, pausing to think aloud, until you've reached the end of your text selection. (For more on which text to choose for modeling, see the section titled, "Choose the Right Text for Modeling," later in this chapter, beginning on Page 30.)

**Encourage Students to Contribute
During the Strategy Modeling Sessions**

Students need to listen and watch your demonstration long enough that they begin to grasp what using these strategies entails. Then they need to get involved. A short way into the lesson, without any encouragement from you, your students will probably begin to raise their hands, perhaps tentatively at first, and then with more vigor. "I have a *connection*," one student may offer. Another student might say, "I think I *figured something out.*"

Happily, there is no one set of "just right" strategies to use to understand text. So welcome your students' contributions during these whole-class strategy-modeling sessions. You can be certain your students will use the comprehension strategies in ways that will not have occurred to you. Each reader filters text through the lens of individual experiences, experiences that may or may not be shared with classmates or shared to varying degrees. *My* use of comprehension strategies will help *me* understand what *I* have read. *Your* strategies will help *you* understand the very same text in a different way. And the strategies Tommy, in the back, left-hand corner of the classroom, chooses to use are perfect for his understanding of the text. As your students gain confidence in using these comprehension strategies, and as they listen to how you use these strategies to understand the text and how their classmates use these strategies, they will begin to experience the value of different points of view in understanding text.

Each time you read a text to the class and then share the thinking strategies you are using to construct meaning from that text, you should see more and more student participation in the think-aloud process. Your students' engagement in the strategy-modeling session tells you that they are beginning to own these thinking processes for themselves.

If your students don't volunteer to share how they are using the strategies to understand the text as they watch and listen while you model these strategies, prompt them to participate with statements like the following: "I'm making a connection here to another book we read. Can anyone think what that connection might be?" Or you might say, "I'm going to read this paragraph again. What picture do these words paint in *your* mind?" Some students need a gentle nudge to get their thinking started.

As you gradually incorporate more and more student responses into your demonstration of comprehension strategies, you are showing your students how to build meaning from the text. This demonstration provides a smooth transition to guided student practice using these strategies, their next step towards independent reading comprehension. Thus begins the transfer of responsibility for using these strategies, from teacher to student.

I believe that one challenge of teaching reading comprehension is that, in our daily lives, teachers, like most adults, don't usually think about how we understand what we read. Instead, because we've engaged in the reading-and-thinking process so many times before, we use these strategies automatically, while we are reading, to understand what we read. Good readers have generally had a lot of experience reading. So they use a range of comprehension strategies flexibly, depending upon the demands of the text as well as their individual style of learning. But the process of building meaning from text is not as automatic for children, who are still learning to read or still learning to read effectively.

Articulate for your students the comprehension strategies you use.

To remedy your students' lack of reading experiences, allow them during the strategy-modeling sessions to "get inside your head." Become aware of your own thought processes while you are reading so you can articulate for your students the comprehension strategies you use before, during, and after reading to understand what you read.

Before reading, show your students how you activate your prior knowledge about the author, the genre of the text, or the topic of the text, how you make predictions about what will happen (if the text is narrative) and what you expect you will learn from the text (if the text is informational). The structure of a text, as well as its illustrations, can inspire readers to guess or predict what will happen. And by so doing, a reader sets a purpose for reading. You may want to enlarge the chart on the next page, so you can display it in the classroom as a reminder to your students of these important pre-reading comprehension strategies. "What to Think about Before Reading" is titled "TwoA" on the CD.

During the modeling session, discuss how good readers, while reading, engage in an internal dialogue with the author of the text, the characters in the text, and other details of the text. You might, for example, pause after the first paragraph you read to say, "Hmmm, I'm wondering here what Hansel and Gretel will do next?" Or "I'm noticing that this poem is by Shel Silverstein. Maybe it will be funny like his other poems." Do not expect perfection with students' strategy use at this point in your reading strategy instruction. It is enough at this stage if your students can

What to Think about Before Reading

1. What do I already know about this topic or this author?

2. What is the genre of this text? What do I know about this genre?

3. What questions will this reading probably answer?

4. Why am I reading this text?

5. What may make this text easy or difficult for me to understand?

6. Will I need to read this text slowly? Or do I expect that I can read it well quickly?

accurately name the strategies (at least most of the time). Later, in teacher-guided practice in small groups (see Chapter Three), your students will have ample opportunity to fine-tune their applications of each and all of these strategies. And you will repeat throughout the coming weeks a cycle of teacher-modeling of strategy use and student practice using the strategies. (See the teaching schedule included in Chapter Three, on pages 55–61.) This cycle of teacher modeling and student practice will move your students to increasing levels of proficiency with their use of all of the comprehension strategies.

Once you reach the conclusion of the text in the modeling session, revisit the predictions and purposes you set before you began reading. Ask your students to help you to determine whether these predictions were accurate. Until students are able to *figure out* how the whole text comes together, class time devoted to teaching reading comprehension strategies will not have achieved its main objective: students' improved reading comprehension.

A Practical Example of Strategy Modeling

If the idea of modeling integrated use of blended comprehension strategies still seems too abstract, the example provided below should give you a thorough lesson in how to model these strategies using a short text.

First, read the text, "The Life and Times of Lily: Memoir of a Mutt" (p. 22. This short story is also available on the CD in the file titled, "TwoB."). You will see, on the pages that follow this short text, how I have used this story to demonstrate integrated use of reading comprehension strategies. I've provided some notes following each text chunk, explaining my rationale for using the comprehension strategies that I used. The strategies I model in this example are those that popped into my head as I constructed meaning from the text. If I were to read this text again, today, I might identify some of the same strategies as useful at each stopping point. But I'd probably incorporate some other strategies, too.

If you would like to use this text in your class, I would recommend it for upper-elementary and middle-school students, but not with primary-grade children. The topic of this piece, a pampered puppy, is fine, but the narrative voice is a bit sophisticated for our youngest students.

The Life and Times of Lily:
Memoir of a Mutt
By Lily

I am NOT a spoiled pup! And I'll yap at you if I you say that I am spoiled! I am very, very cute and also cuddly! And the people I live with practically trip over themselves catering to my every whim. There's no little house in the backyard or crate in the kitchen for me to sleep in! Oh, no! I put my pretty little head down each night between two king-size pillows on little Caitlin's bed. And most of the time, I leave room for Caitlin, too. "Two princesses," her Mom and Dad say when they tuck us in each night and turn out the light.

The other princess has long black hair and shiny metal things on her teeth. My hair is a beautiful apricot color, and my teeth work fine just the way they are! I don't need any shiny things to fix my teeth. Maybe my teeth work too well! Caitlin's mom is always telling me, "Don't chew the woodwork, Lily....Don't chew the chair leg, Lily." Mom has too many RULES!

Her worst rule is that I am not allowed to eat people food! The people in my family get good stuff out of the oven that looks yummy and smells great, too. But I, on the other hand (or other paw, as someone of my species would say), I get mystery-mush out of a can that reads, Alpo. (Bet you didn't know I can read, did you? But how could I write if I couldn't read?)

Anyway, Mom's rule about me not getting people food is NOT FAIR! So I whimper and whine every night at suppertime. But then Dad says, "Hush, Lily, or I'll put you in Caitlin's room until dinner is over." Then I quiet down and hide under the table. I curl up my furry, five-pound body into a quiet little ball and pretend to be asleep. But really, I'm waiting for someone to drop something tasty. And if I'm patient, I almost always get lucky. Last night, I got a French fry. And the night before, I got a bite of chicken! There's always a little bit of people food falling somewhere near the table!

And after dinner, Dad sometimes gives me a doggie treat. But I usually have to work much too hard for it. Here's what I mean: One night, Dad seemed DETERMINED to teach me to sit. But I already know perfectly well how to sit. I just don't like to do it when he wants me to. So before he would give me a doggie-treat that night, he began telling me, "Sit, Lily. Sit!" He said this in a very commanding tone, over and over again. But I just stood there, pretending not to know what he wanted me to do. Oh, I knew what he wanted me to do, all right. But that kitchen tile was way too cold and much too hard for my Pomeranian backside. But Dad just wouldn't give up.

"Watch me!" he finally sighed. And so I watched while he climbed down onto that cold, hard tile floor and crawled toward me on all fours. Then he squatted in front of me, saying, "Just like this, Lily! Sit!" There he was, this big, bald man, actually demonstrating to me how to sit, doggie style! It was very funny!

So I said, "Woof! Woof! Woof!" And Dad answered, but I didn't quite catch what he said.

Words you would say to students appear in italics. The "thinking behind the thinking" is in parentheses following each bulleted point.

Read Aloud the Title, Subtitle, and Author
THE LIFE AND TIMES OF LILY
Memoir of a Mutt
By Lily

Think Aloud about the Title, Subtitle, and Author

• *Before beginning to read this text, let's see if there are any clues in the title, or if I know anything about the author. Well, I'm **noticing** that this piece of text is about Lily, and it's also by Lily. The author is writing about herself. I'm also noticing that Lily doesn't have a last name. That's a little weird.*

> (We want to show students that good readers look carefully at the title, the author's name, any illustration on the front cover, and anything else that can provide clues to the meaning of the text before we begin to read the text itself.)

• *I'm **noticing** that this is a memoir, which means it tells about someone's life experiences. But it may not have everything in it that a story has — like a problem and a solution.*

> (We want students to activate prior knowledge about the genre as it helps them to predict the structure of the text.)

• *I'm **noticing** too that it says "memoir of a mutt." I know that a mutt is a dog, so Lily couldn't have really written this about herself. I'm **guessing** that the author is probably writing this from Lily's point of view.*

> (In this case, we are showing students that good readers make predictions before they read. These predictions help us to read purposefully as we want to find out whether our predictions were accurate.)

• *I know already that I can make some **connections** to this text because I have a dog. Sometimes she has some pretty crazy adventures. But I love her anyway. I **wonder** if Lily is anything like my dog.*

> (It's important for students to see that good readers look for connections. Connections provide a sense of kinship with the author and with the text. And connections lead to the kind of questioning that generates critical thinking.)

• *As I read this memoir, I'm going to try to **figure out** why the author wrote about this dog.*

(Before beginning to read, good readers set a purpose for themselves. Really good readers are already thinking about the author's purpose, too. This kind of *figuring out* leads ultimately to an understanding of theme.)

Read Aloud the First Chunk of Text

I am NOT a spoiled pup! And I'll yap at you if I you say that I am spoiled! I am very, very cute and also cuddly! And the people I live with practically trip over themselves catering to my every whim. There's no little house in the backyard or crate in the kitchen for me to sleep in! Oh, no! I put my pretty little head down each night between two king-size pillows on little Caitlin's bed. And most of the time, I leave room for Caitlin, too. "Two princesses," her Mom and Dad say when they tuck us in each night and turn out the light.

Think Aloud about the First Chunk of Text

- *I'm **noticing** that I was right about the author writing this memoir from the dog's point of view.*

 (We're showing students here that good readers self-monitor. Before reading, I guessed, or predicted, that the author was using the dog's voice to tell this tale. Now I see that my thinking was right on-target.)

- *I'm **figuring out** that this dog really is spoiled, even though she says she isn't. I have proof: Her people wait on her. She sleeps on a "people bed" between big pillows, and she is called "a princess."*

 (As a good reader, I can draw my own conclusions, even when the author doesn't tell me something directly. I'm also demonstrating to the students that good readers go back to the text to locate evidence for their opinions.)

- *I can also **figure out** that this must be a small dog. The author says she sleeps between two pillows on Caitlin's bed; she'd have to be small to do that. I **wonder** what kind of dog this is. And who is Caitlin? Maybe I'll find out if I keep reading.*

 (I'm drawing another conclusion from the important clues in the text. The author doesn't *say* that this is a small dog, but she *shows* this by providing the detail about the two pillows. Wondering about the breed of the dog and the identity of the "other princess" will keep me reading.)

- *The author is describing a scene here, so it's a good place for me to try to make a picture in my mind. I can **picture** this whole scene. I bet this bed has really puffy pillows with frilly, pink pillowcases. In my mind, Lily looks kind of like a Beanie Baby with her nose poked out* *from between lots of pink lace. She probably has a collar with sparkly sequins and beads on it.*

> (Note here that the picture I've created in my mind goes along with the "princess" theme, and I've moved beyond the words in the text to create this picture. Students need to see that visualizing is more than retelling. If we want this scene to be memorable, it needs good elaboration.)

Read Aloud the Second Chunk of Text

The other princess has long black hair and shiny metal things on her teeth. My hair is a beautiful apricot color, and my teeth work fine just the way they are! I don't need any shiny things to fix my teeth. Maybe my teeth work too well! Caitlin's mom is always telling me, "Don't chew the woodwork, Lily….Don't chew the chair leg, Lily." Mom has too many RULES!

Think Aloud about the Second Chunk of Text

- *I'm **guessing** that "the other princess" — Caitlin — might be a teenager. Those "shiny metal things" could be braces; I know that sometimes teenagers have braces. I **wonder** if the author will give me some more clues about Caitlin as I continue to read.*

  > (Good readers take chances with their comprehension of the text. They form a hypothesis and continue their reading carefully in order to confirm or disconfirm their predictions.)

- *I can get a picture in my mind of Mom. She's probably standing there shaking her finger at Lily, looking at the chewed woodwork. I can hear her voice, too: Bossy!*

  > (In this case, *picturing* involves hearing as well as seeing. Readers need to be reminded that using all of their senses helps to make the pictures in their mind more memorable.)

- *I **notice** that the author wrote the word "RULES" in upper case letters. Mom's rules must be important. I **wonder** if the author is going to tell me more about Mom's rules.*

  > (Highlighting specific words by changing the font or capitalizing them is an example of author's craft. Good readers read with a writer's eye and recognize that this word has been highlighted for a reason.)

Read Aloud the Third Chunk of Text

Her worst rule is that I am not allowed to eat people food! The people in my family get good stuff out of the oven that looks yummy and smells great, too. But I, on the other hand (or other paw, as someone of my species would say), I get mystery-mush out of a can that reads, *Alpo*. (Bet you didn't know I can read, did you? But how could I write if I couldn't read?)

Think Aloud about the Third Chunk of Text

- *I'm **noticing** that the author is telling me more about Mom's rules.*
  (Good monitoring here! Now I know that the author did use those upper-case letters for a reason.)
- *I can make a **connection** here, too. My friend has a dog, and she always feeds it from the table. Now that dog won't eat her dog food. And she is getting chubby. I know why Mom has this rule.*
  (Note that this connection goes beyond a parallel experience. It led to an understanding of a character's possible motives.)
- *I'm **picturing** that Alpo can with those smiling dogs on the front of it. But, like Lily, I wouldn't be happy if I had to eat something that looked and smelled like that!*
  (Name brands such as *Alpo* make *picturing* easy. They flood the mind with instant memories.)

Read Aloud the Fourth Chunk of Text

Anyway, Mom's rule about me not getting people food is NOT FAIR! So I whimper and whine every night at suppertime. But then Dad says, "Hush, Lily, or I'll put you in Caitlin's room until dinner is over." Then I quiet down and hide under the table. I curl up my furry, five-pound body into a quiet little ball and pretend to be asleep. But really, I'm waiting for someone to drop something tasty. And if I'm patient, I almost always get lucky. Last night, I got a French fry. And the night before, I got a bite of chicken! There's always a little bit of people food falling somewhere near the table!

Think Aloud about the Fourth Chunk of Text

- *I'm **noticing** more clues about the dog. She really is little: only five pounds! Now I know that Lily is a miniature dog with long, fluffy hair. Unfortunately I don't know that much about dogs, so I still don't know the breed.*
  (Good readers know to file away clues as they read so that they can eventually synthesize them. However, when readers don't have sufficient background knowledge, even noticing all the best clues isn't enough to construct meaning. In this case, if the author doesn't eventually clarify the breed, it will forever remain a mystery for this reader.)

Good readers form a hypothesis and continue reading carefully to confirm or discount those predictions.

- *I'm **noticing** that I'm meeting a new character here: Dad. I don't know much about him yet.*
- *I **wonder** if I'll get to know him better in the next part that I read.*
    (Understanding characters is central to understanding the meaning of a text. We always want our readers to notice characters as they are introduced. We want them to be "on the look out" for character traits.)

Read Aloud the Fifth Chunk of Text

And after dinner, Dad sometimes gives me a doggie treat. But I usually have to work much too hard for it. Here's what I mean: One night, Dad seemed DETERMINED to teach me to sit. But I already know perfectly well how to sit. I just don't like to do it when he wants me to. So before he would give me a doggie-treat that night, he began telling me, "Sit, Lily. Sit!" He said this in a very commanding tone, over and over again. But I just stood there, pretending not to know what he wanted me to do. Oh, I knew what he wanted me to do, all right. But that kitchen tile was way too cold and much too hard for my Pomeranian backside. But Dad just wouldn't give up.

Think Aloud about the Fifth Chunk of Text

- *I'm **noticing** that I <u>am</u> learning a lot more about Dad. He is very nice to Lily and spends time trying to teach her things.*
    (More monitoring. This is a good snapshot of Dad, and the reader is aware of it.)
- *I'm also **noticing** that this is a Pomeranian. Maybe I can find a picture of this kind of dog so I will really know what it looks like.*
    (Close reading increases a reader's schema, or background knowledge. The reader will be able to bring this new knowledge to future reading about dogs.)

Read Aloud the Last Chunk of Text

"Watch me!" he finally sighed. And so I watched while he climbed down onto that cold, hard tile floor and crawled toward me on all fours. Then he squatted in front of me, saying, "Like this, Lily! Sit!" There he was, this big, bald man, actually demonstrating to me how to sit, doggie style! It was very funny!

So I said, "Woof! Woof! Woof!" And Dad answered, but I didn't quite catch what he said.

Think Aloud about the Last Chunk of Text

- *I've got a great **picture** in my mind of Dad crawling around on the floor like a dog. I see this big, bald man in jeans and a T-shirt creeping toward the dog, pretending he actually <u>is</u> a dog. The dog is looking at him like he doesn't believe a grown man would do this.*

(This vignette practically *begs* the reader to create a mental image. There are lots of details here awaiting the reader's interpretation.)

- *I **wonder** what Dad said to the dog at the end? This is the end of the reading, so I'll never know for sure. But I'm **guessing** he might be losing his patience.*

    (Authors often leave the reader with something to ponder. Although Dad's response is not indicated, good readers will infer that Dad was probably not saying something complimentary to Lily.)

- *Going back to my purpose for reading, I'm **figuring out** that the author wrote this to show that this family really loves Lily. Even though she's kind of a princess and begs for people food, and won't obey, they still think she's the most wonderful dog in the world.*

    (Good readers always return to their purpose when they have finished their reading. They try to decide how everything fits together. They try to figure out why the author has written the piece, and what the message or theme might be.)

You will probably want to model your use of all the comprehension strategies several times before turning over to your students more responsibility for strategic thinking while they read. When you feel your students are ready to assume more responsibility for using these comprehension strategies while reading, you can move from modeling your use of these strategies in front of the whole class to small-group work, where each student has the opportunity to try out this Read-Aloud/Think-Aloud process for herself.

Using the entire repertoire of strategies promoted comprehension of this text beyond what could have been achieved through a focus on only one strategy. For example, if we had focused exclusively on *picturing* we would have finished our reading with several multi-sensory snapshots featuring Lily. But we would have overlooked the *connections* that provided insights into characters. And we would have missed some great opportunities to *figure out* features of this story that needed to be inferred or synthesized.

Although this text was short, only a few paragraphs, it presented numerous occasions to model multiple strategies.

Choose the Right Text for Modeling

Your choice of text will be critical to your success in modeling reading comprehension strategies. There's a lot to consider when you select a text for a strategy-modeling session. But since you will be doing the reading, out loud, to your entire class, the developmental reading level of the text you choose will be less of a factor than if your students were reading the material, rather than listening to you read (and listening to you think out loud about what you read.)

I truly believe that opportunities for demonstrating the use of every reading comprehension strategy abound in every text. In every text — whether a poem, a picture book, a short story, an article from a newspaper, magazine or textbook, or an excerpt from a longer work of fiction or nonfiction — you will find ideas, words, and many details that help readers construct meaning as they activate comprehension strategies.

The list of books I have included below, beginning on Page 33, contains the titles of 29 texts that invite thinking across all the comprehension strategies. Some of the texts in this list are ideal for primary-grade students, and other texts in this list address the interests of older readers. Especially as you begin to model reading comprehension strategies for your class, I encourage you to make selections from this list. But generally, as you become more comfortable choosing texts for modeling reading strategies, you will want to keep in mind the following considerations:

- **Keep It Short**
  Whatever text you choose to use in your strategy-modeling sessions, short texts work best. Choose a text that you can read to your class comfortably, in one sitting or two, taking into consideration the additional time necessary to discuss your use of comprehension strategies while you read out loud to your class. Keep in mind that what qualifies as *short* will vary depending upon the age and grade level for whom you are modeling the strategies; what is considered a "single sitting" for first graders will be more brief than what may be a "single sitting" for an older student.

- **Use Picture Books**
  Picture books are especially well suited for modeling reading strategies. I like using picture books for strategy-modeling sessions because the illustrations offer an additional, non-textual focus for modeling a range of strategies. Additionally, illustrations demonstrate how the book's illustrator has applied the *picturing* strategy to understand the text. Referring to illustrations is not, of course, the

only way to help children learn to use the *picturing* strategy. Books with vivid language allow attentive readers (or, in the case of your strategy-modeling sessions, attentive listeners) to create powerful mental images.

- **Use Pre-chunked Text (Or "Chunk" Your Own)**
One other advantage of using a picture book to model reading strategies for your class is that the text in picture books comes "pre-chunked," my invented term for text that is already segmented into the bite-sized portions that are best for modeling reading strategies. Poetry, too, will often come in this "pre-chunked" format since many poems are divided into short stanzas. (But when choosing poems for your strategy-modeling sessions, avoid any poems where the sound or rhythms of the language and phrases contributes heavily to the overall meaning of the poem. Such poems will not be good choices for your Read-Aloud/Think-Aloud sessions since the beauty of the language will be lost as you interrupt the reading to discuss your thinking strategies.)

If you choose a text that is not "pre-chunked," such as a short story, decide before you begin your modeling session where in the text you will pause to think out loud about the comprehension strategies you use to construct meaning from the text.

With many short texts, such as some poems or with excerpts from informational text, I use an overhead projector to demonstrate to students the process of "marking up a text" to note which strategies I have used and where I used them. Since some students benefit from *seeing* the text in addition to *hearing* it, use of an overhead projector can help address the needs of these students who learn best visually.

- **Consider "Connectability" and the Level of Challenge**
I have learned (the hard way) that a strategy-modeling session is much more likely to engage students, and they, therefore, are more likely to learn how to use reading comprehension strategies, if I choose a text carefully matched to students' interests. Find a text that addresses a topic to which your students are likely to connect in a significant way.

Subjects that seem to work well in strategy-modeling sessions often involve real kids solving real problems. The emphasis in such texts is usually character development, which offers rich possibilities for strategic thinking. Books that are useful for text-to-self connections contain common themes universal to childhood, such as friendship, sibling relationships, school issues, fear, jealousy, feeling different and other matters related to growing up. And while girls sometimes

Opportunities for demonstrating the use of every reading comprehension strategy abound in every text.

don't want to hear stories with *boy* main characters, and boys sometimes object to stories about "girl stuff," almost everyone (including adults) enjoys reading about animals, particularly dogs.

Stories packed with adventure or very humorous texts are sometimes not good choices for modeling comprehension strategies. Kids so enjoy the thrill or the laughs of such stories that they are likely to monitor their comprehension even without your encouragement. The best texts to use in these sessions are those that are interesting and engaging, but also a bit challenging. As you assess the value of a potential text for strategy modeling, ask yourself, "Will my students reach a deeper understanding and appreciation of this text if we study it together?" If the answer is "yes," then the selection is probably appropriate.

The texts identified in the following brief, annotated bibliography are some are some of my favorites for modeling a repertoire of comprehension strategies at primary, intermediate-grade, and upper-elementary-grade levels.

• **Model Individual Strategy Applications Later On**
You will want your early strategy-modeling sessions to focus on the integrated use of several comprehension strategies. Later on, after you've had the chance to assess your students' abilities to use these strategies during small-group practice (See Chapter Three), you will be able to determine which individual reading strategies to target in strategy-modeling sessions. At that point, you can model the specific applications of individual strategies (Chapter Seven). And you may want to note texts that seem better suited to modeling the application of one strategy over another strategy. You will find in the annotated bibliography beginning on page 198, a guide for picture books that are particularly well-suited to such targeted strategy-application modeling.

The texts identified in the following brief, annotated bibliography are some of my favorites for modeling a repertoire of comprehension strategies at primary, intermediate grade, and upper elementary and middle school levels.

Texts Well Suited for Modeling
Reading Comprehension Strategies

For Younger Students

A Chair for My Mother by Vera Williams, New York: Greenwillow Books,
  1982.
  A family works together to save for something special after a fire destroys
  their home. Shows the love and mutual respect of an extended family.

Alexander and the Terrible, Horrible, No Good, Very Bad Day by Judith Viorst,
  New York: Simon and Schuster, 1972.
  Kids readily relate to the idea of a "very bad day" (teachers too!).

Dandelion by Don Freeman, New York: Puffin Books, 1977.
  This very simple story reminds children of the consequences of vanity.

Koala Lou by Mem Fox, New York: Harcourt Brace & Company, 1989.
  Kids can *figure out* from this animal tale that a parent's love is ever-
  present, not something that must be earned.

Pigsty by Mark Teague, New York: Scholastic, 1994.
  Children can relate to this comical story of a very messy bedroom.

Tacky the Penguin by Helen Lester, Boston: Houghton Mifflin, 1988.
  Tacky was an "odd bird." But, in the end, his unwillingness to follow the
  pack saved the day.

The Bracelet by Yoshiko Uchida, New York: Philomel Books, 1993.
  This book about Japanese internment camps offers insights into the
  meaning of friendship.

The Legend of the Bluebonnet by Tomie DePaola, New York: Scholastic, 1983.
  This Native American folktale tells of a little girl who gives up her most
  valued possession to save her People.

The Rainbow Fish by Marcus Pfister, New York: North-South Books, 1992.
  A fable about the joy of giving.

Too Many Tamales by Gary Soto, New York: Scholastic, 1993.
  Provides many opportunities to use all strategies, but may be especially
  helpful in encouraging students to predict: How will Mama finally get
  her diamond ring back?

For Intermediate-Grade Students

A Bad Case of Stripes by David Shannon, New York: Scholastic, 1998.
  Camilla Cream is too concerned with the opinions of her friends to stand
  up for what she wants. She comes down with a strange ailment and isn't
  cured until she admits her secret passion (a love of lima beans!).

Dear Mrs. LaRue: Letters from Obedience School by Mark Teague, New York: Scholastic, 2002.

This funny story, written in the voice of Ike, the dog, will get readers thinking about how Ike's bad habits may serve a useful purpose. Encourage your students to find the clues the author provides.

Fables by Arnold Lobel, New York: Harper and Row, 1980.

These fables have a modern, funny twist, and students of all ages love them.

Knots on a Counting Rope by Bill Martin Jr. and John Archambault, New York: Henry Holt and Company, 1987.

In this tale of intergenerational love and respect, a grandfather helps his grandson face his greatest challenge: blindness. The story helps children ponder their own special challenges and how they can face them.

My Rotten Redheaded Older Brother by Patricia Polacco, New York: Simon and Schuster, 1994.

Competition between siblings is the theme of this story about a kid who wants to do something, *anything*, better than big brother.

Salt in His Shoes: Michael Jordan in Pursuit of a Dream by Deloris Jordan, New York: Simon and Schuster, 2000.

The mother of basketball superstar Michael Jordan shares her recollections of her son's pursuit of his dream in the face of adversity. The story offers a message of hope, faith, and family togetherness.

Snowflake Bentley by Jacqueline Briggs Martin, Boston: Houghton Mifflin, 1998.

Wilson Bentley, often misunderstood in his own time, perceived snowflakes as small miracles. His photography captured beautiful images of snowflakes. And his story demonstrates both a scientist's vision and a personal passion for nature. Caldecott Award.

Something Beautiful by Sharon Dennis Wyeth, New York: Bantam Doubleday Dell, 1998.

We can find beauty in our world regardless of our circumstances. The illustrations here are as powerful as the words.

The Paper Bag Princess by Robert Munsch, New York: Firefly Books, 1980.

This fairy tale with a "strong girl" theme is enjoyed by readers of all ages and dispels the stereotypic "princess" image.

The Summer My Father was Ten by Pat Brisson, Honesdale (PA): Boyds Mills Press, 1998.

Intergenerational friendship grows out of a thoughtless childhood deed.

For Upper-Elementary and Middle-School Students

Dear Mother, Dear Daughter by Jane Yolen and Heidi E. Y. Stemple, Honesdale, PA: Boyds Mills Press, 2001.

The poems in this little volume by Jane Yolen and her daughter are written as a series of letters from mother to daughter and from daughter to mother around topics that are perennial favorites in a parent-child relationship: cleaning your bedroom, doing homework, talking on the phone, etc. These poems are excellent for teaching point-of-view in a piece of literature.

Every Living Thing by Cynthia Rylant, New York: Simon and Schuster, 1985.

My all-time-favorite anthology of short stories is this thin volume, which contains 12 stories, all featuring animals in a central way. Stories vary a bit in level of sophistication.

Faithful Elephants by Yukio Tsuchiya, Boston: Houghton Mifflin, 1988.

Issues related to the devastating effects of war on *all* living creatures. For older readers.

Pink and Say by Patricia Polacco, New York: Scholastic, 1994.

This book addresses treatment of African Americans in the South during the Civil War and is a touching story of friendship.

The Rough-Face Girl by Rafe Martin, New York: Puffin Books, 1992.

In this Algonquin Cinderella, readers discover that a scarred face can't disguise the beauty and kindness of this girl's heart.

The Royal Bee by Frances Park and Ginger Park, Honesdale (PA): Boyds Mills Press, 2000.

A poor Korean boy finds a way to receive an education and goes on to win a national award for his courage and intelligence. Encourages children to consider the value of receiving an education.

The Three Questions (based on a story by Leo Tolstoy) by Jon Muth, New York: Scholastic, 2002.

In this text, three important questions are asked: When is the best time to do things? Who is most important? What is the right thing to do? This is a beautifully illustrated story with an even more beautiful message.

The Wretched Stone by Chris Van Allsburg, Boston: Houghton Mifflin, 1991.

The author provides clues throughout the text so the reader can determine the identity of "the wretched stone." This story is excellent for kids who can think abstractly.

Wings by Christopher Myers, New York: Scholastic, 2000.

Main character is Ikarus Jackson, who uses his beautiful wings to fly — despite the scorn he faces from peers for being so different. Lends itself to questions about embracing our differences and celebrating our individuality.

These texts are some of my favorites for modeling a repertoire of strategies.

3

Guided Student Practice:
Using Comprehension Strategies
in a Small Group

All attributes of this instructional model are effective in a small-group setting, where instruction is intensive, integrated, and interactive. And a small group, in which participants have a similar reading level, is ideal for student practice using multiple reading comprehension strategies.

Students need plenty of time to *practice* comprehension strategies in a small group after they've heard the strategies explained and watched their teacher modeling use of these strategies for the whole class.

Practicing the integrated use of reading comprehension strategies in a small group setting is highly engaging for students.

Student practice with reading strategies among peers in a small group helps students to value their own thinking strategies and that of their peers, and it leads to a successful transfer of responsibility for learning from teacher to student.

In too many instances, instruction in reading comprehension has focused on what and how the *teacher* is thinking. The teacher asks a question, gets the answer she wants, and moves on to the next question. In such a teaching format, a student succeeds, not by elaborating on what is in his or her own mind, but by correctly guessing what is on the teacher's mind.

This more traditional method of teaching reading does not encourage teacher and students to collaborate in the construction of meaning from text. There is little authentic dialogue.

But in this small-group practice activity, the teacher's role is not that of a "question dispenser;" she is a learned member of the group. She is alert to point to what would benefit from clarification. She knows when to model her own thinking for her students and when to nudge her students' thinking forward in an open-ended way, such as, "I'm getting a great picture in my mind here. Is anyone else able to get a mental image of this scene?" Such prompts from the teacher encourage divergent responses from students, not a one-size-fits-all answer.

In this kind of small-group practice session, as the teacher shares with the rest of the group her *connections* to the text, what she *notices* when she reads the text, her point of view carries no more authority than the insights offered by any of the other students in the small group. And in this way, the small-group-discussion format for these strategy-practice sessions allows students and teacher to truly collaborate as meaning-makers, to use each other's insights to confirm, contrast, modify, or extend their own understanding of the text.

And most importantly, when the teacher's voice is one of several voices contributing to the understanding of a text, students are more likely to value and explore their own thinking processes (and the differing points of view held by their peers, too). Students begin to feel confident using these strategies to think actively while they read. They are not so worried about being "wrong" because they are reflecting on their own thought processes rather than on questions with right and wrong answers.

I hope this chapter will help you, as a teacher, visualize how student practice of integrated reading comprehension strategies might look in your classroom. You will need to adapt the example I provide in this chapter to the ages or reading levels in your class. For a selection of books that are especially well suited to small-group guided practice using reading comprehension strategies, see "Anthologies of Short Stories and Books of Poetry," page 218.

At this stage in your reading strategy instruction, you will already have provided your students with an initial explanation of comprehension strategies (see Chapter One). Then you conducted one or more whole-group lessons, modeling use of the reading strategies with the *Lily* story and other texts, too (see Chapter Two).

Now you gather a small group of students to practice these strategies with you.

Necessity of Small Group Setting for Student Practice of Reading Comprehension Strategies

As any teacher knows, when we conduct whole-class instruction, some students participate enthusiastically, and we may have a great discussion going on. This interaction can provide opportunities to demonstrate or discuss a topic for the whole class. And it allows the teacher to assess how the most vocal students in the class are handling the material. In such a setting, it may be easy to see that Sarah makes great inferences, but she has trouble synthesizing. And you can tell that Jamal likes to be part of the discussion although his thinking is generally superficial.

But what about the rest of the students? A teacher cannot be certain that the "nonparticipators" in the class are quietly taking everything in and just keeping their thoughts to themselves. These quiet students might, instead, be contemplating the soccer game they intend to play after school. And even as students begin to share their own thinking strategies during the teacher-modeling sessions, teachers have no way during the whole-class sessions to assess how or even whether the less verbal students in the class are using all or any of the reading comprehension strategies.

If we want classroom practice to truly move *all* students toward independence, we need to allow students to practice these strategies with the teacher in a small group, the setting that best allows students to participate fully and to interact with the teacher and their peers. This setting also allows the teacher to accurately assess the ability of each student to use the reading strategies.

Sometimes students are so disconnected from what they read that they appear not to comprehend the text, although they do have the ability to comprehend well. The small-group practice format keeps all the students in the small group actively engaged in the text. They remain focused because they know they will be expected to explain their thinking strategy after reading each chunk of text. They also are more likely to participate willingly in the conversation because their insights and points of view are invited, heard, and discussed.

Optimal Number of Students to Include
in Small Group Practice Sessions

The number of students to include in a small group should be determined primarily by two considerations. The size of the group must allow each student the opportunity to participate fully in the strategy-practice activity. It must also allow the teacher to thoroughly monitor the ability of each student in the small group to use these strategies. To the extent that the small-group size meets both of these criteria, the optimal number of students is negotiable.

Four to six students in a group generally works well at the early primary level or with struggling readers. With older students, the group can remain effective with even seven or eight students, especially when students are reading at a level that is average or better for their grade level.

Regardless of the grade or ability level, bear in mind that you want to keep the size of your group small enough so that all of its members *willingly* participate. Some children just don't feel comfortable joining the conversation when they perceive that the group is too big and there's too much risk involved.

Need for Comparable Reading Levels in Small Groups

It's generally a good practice to provide opportunities within the school day for many different classroom groupings. But for the purpose of students practicing reading comprehension strategies in a small group, reading proficiency should, to a large extent, dictate how students are grouped.

For best results in these small-group practice sessions, all the students in the group should be reading at a comparable instructional level. "Instructional level" is that level at which a student is challenged enough by the text to experience the value of using the comprehension strategies, but not so challenged that acquiring meaning from the text becomes frustrating. The text will almost certainly frustrate students if there are more than two or three words per page that they do not recognize.

You can, however, have a successful small-group practice session with a group of students who are at differing instructional reading levels *if* the students in the group have similar background knowledge of the subject of the text and *if* the teacher is willing to provide extra scaffolding. Even

If we monitor students' performance carefully, these groups will change members frequently.

in that scenario, however, the children grouped together must, at a minimum, all be able to *decode* the text.

If we monitor students' performance carefully, these groups will change frequently. We will recognize which students are able to describe their thinking about a text with ease and which students struggle with even basic comprehension. Then we can re-group children with other readers who demonstrate similar needs for the next round of strategy practice.

Arranging Classroom Activities and Furnishings to Support Small Group Practice Sessions

This approach to guided comprehension-strategy practice does not involve a lot of written planning. Reading the text prior to the lesson and taking notes on thinking strategies that might be used for each text segment is, of course, crucial. But no long paper trail, expensive kits nor massive anthologies are required. However, other kinds of planning are necessary to the success of this method.

Many teachers tell me, "It's not the small group that's the problem — it's the other eighteen kids who are sitting at their desks. What will *they* do when I am chatting about a book in a small group?"

Chapter Seven addresses how to position comprehension strategy instruction at the heart of a comprehensive literacy program. Independent reading activities and other literacy-related work can keep students engaged at their seats while other students participate in a guided reading group with the teacher.

But small-group instruction is so important to your students' literacy success that devising a teaching plan (and a furniture arrangement) to make these sessions work in your classroom is worth whatever effort is necessary. Ultimately, each teacher must come up with a plan that works well in his or her classroom to organize student activities so that small-group practice sessions with the teacher can take place with little or no interruption while the rest of the class is engaged in independent student work.

You will need a place in your classroom to meet with your small group, a space set apart from the rest of the class. It's helpful in this small-group activity if students can be seated around a table. But the activity also works with students sitting in a circle on a rug, perhaps in the library corner of your classroom, an area that may already be designated for small-group work.

What we're trying to achieve in these sessions is the look and feel of a book chat around the dining room table with a group of friends or family members. The format you choose for these strategy-practice sessions is intended to simulate the way experienced readers think about and discuss their reading. These sessions might even get a little noisy. People who are exited about what they've read engage in lively discussion about the *connections* to characters they've discovered, the *questions* that remain unanswered, and the scenes they can *picture* in their mind. Their talk about text is passionate and animated. And your students will begin to discuss what they read in this way, too as the instructional format becomes more collaborative and less teacher-directed.

Procedures for Strategy Instruction in Small Groups

Once you have gathered the number of children you want to participate in your small group, and you and your group are settled comfortably in a special place in your classroom, you can begin the small group strategy-practice session.

- **Begin by passing out a large, blank index card to each student.**
"Here's a big index card for each of you," I might tell the students at this time. "Use it to cover up the part of the text we haven't read yet."

I don't want students to read ahead of the chunk of text we're currently discussing. If I expect students to make predictions as they read and use other reading strategies to monitor their understanding of the text, they must not race ahead, from line to line, on their own.

- **Next, distribute to each student a copy of the text the group will read together.**
Sometimes I choose a short story. Sometimes I use an excerpt from a longer text. Sometimes I select a poem. (For more ideas, review again my list of suggested texts on pages 33–35 in Chapter Two and in the annotated bibliography beginning on page 198.) For this example, I'm using a poem, "The Sleepover," by Betsy Franco, taken from the small poetry anthology *Miles of Smiles* (Bruce Lansky, Ed.) This short, five-stanza poem is perfect for students in the intermediate grades. Nine- or ten-year-olds especially are cutting-edge authorities on the subject of sleepover parties. So I anticipate a lot of connections when I use this poem with that age group.

- **Next, place two sets of laminated reading-strategy cue cards within easy reach of the students in your group,** whether your group is seated around a table or in a circle on the floor. (You will find materials to make these cards on page 245 and in the file titled, "ThreeA1," on the CD inside the back cover).

These cue cards will help your students to grasp (both literally and figuratively) abstract ideas about how they think when they read. Not all students are auditory learners, and many students have difficulty processing abstract concepts. The cognitive strategies you want them to become comfortable using might, especially at first, seem challenging. These laminated cue-cards provide students with a sensory tool that help them practice using these strategies. In the small-group practice sessions, students select and hold these cards as a visual and tactile reference to the reading comprehension strategies they are using.

"What are these?" I ask as I place the cue-cards face up in the center of the group.

"These are the reading strategies we've been learning about," someone may answer.

Sometimes kids will grab for a particular card, perhaps the *Connecting* card or the *Wondering* card. Sometimes they will try to line up the cards in some prescribed order. Sometimes they flip the cards face down, as if we're going to play a card game! As I watch their behavior with the cue-cards, as I have done so often over the years, I guess they are trying to organize what does not yet make much sense to them.

"Let's leave the cards face-side-up, in the center," I suggest. "Everyone gets to use *all* of the cards."

Sometimes kids come to this experience with prior knowledge of the literature-circle model, in which students have individual roles, as in Word Wizard, Passage Picker, etc. But in this activity, each student will integrate multiple reading comprehension strategies, or roles.

- **Model the practice activity for the small group.**

"Watch how I do this," I begin. "I'm going to read the first chunk of text, the title. Then I will look at the strategy cards in front of me and think about which strategy is helping me to understand what I just read."

I demonstrate: " 'The Sleepover,' " I read out loud.

After a pause as I look over the cue-cards, I then pick up the *Wondering* card and hold it in front of me so all the students can see the reading strategy I've chosen.

"OK," I tell them. "I'm *wondering* if this text is going to be about a party where kids stay at a friend's house overnight. I'm *wondering* if it's going to be a wild and crazy time like sleepover parties I had at my house sometimes when I was a kid. I'm *wondering* if the parents in this story are going to get mad, like my parents did sometimes, when things got out of hand at my sleepover parties. As I read the poem, I'm going to look for answers to these questions."

I pause and scan the faces of the children in front of me. "What did you see me do here?" I ask. And perhaps a student will answer, "You picked up the strategy card with the name of the strategy you were using." Another student may add, "You said *how* you were using that strategy."

"Yes," I reply. "I chose a strategy and I said how I used it. I also said how I expect the strategy will help me to understand the rest of the poem."

Encourage your students to check from time to time to see whether their reading-strategy choices are leading to a better understanding of what they read. To help them make this connection between using the strategies and better understanding of the text, the teacher should identify the explicit connection between any strategy and the resulting comprehension of the text. If a teacher does not make this connection explicit, students may conclude, incorrectly, that the instructional goal is *only* identifying reading comprehension strategies, rather than using these strategies to understand the text.

Encourage them to make the connection between using the strategies and better understanding of the text.

- **Allow students to begin to practice the strategies.**

"Now I want *you* to do the same thing with the first stanza of the poem," I tell the students. "Let's all read the first stanza of this poem. As you read it, think about a strategy that is helping you to understand this stanza. Then pick up the card that names that strategy and hold the card in front of you. After everyone in the group has a card, we will then each share our strategy thinking, one at a time."

I can usually tell by the students' eyes that they *think* they get the general idea, but they're not quite *sure*.

If you know how well the students read, let them read the text *silently* since that is how more mature readers read when trying to comprehend a text. Somteimes when I visit a classroom to introduce strategies I ask the students to read orally in unison since I am unsure about their level of expertise.

In this example, we read aloud, together, the first stanza, as a chorus:

> *My dad approved an overnight,*
> *I promised we would sleep —*
> *that after ten o'clock at night,*
> *he wouldn't hear a peep.*

Then we stop reading. I stifle the urge to offer my young scholars more "advice" on using the reading strategies. Instead, I let them reflect on their thinking without interruption from me.

I see eyes darting from one strategy cue-card to another. Willy's tentative hand reaches for the *Noticing* card, but then he withdraws it, making a lunge for *Wondering*. However, Makayla is quicker, and she gets the *Wondering* card. When Willy realizes that the second W*ondering* card has also been scooped up, he returns to his original choice, *Noticing*. Everyone is now holding a strategy cue-card except Devon. I wait another few seconds for him to make his selection. He does. Then I grab the remaining *Noticing* card, so I can add my voice to this conversation.

All of my strategy teaching this morning — the definitions, explanation and modeling — has been building to this moment. This is the point at which students begin to own the reading strategies, to assimilate the knowledge they've acquired thus far and apply it themselves.

While I try to convey an air of confidence about their ability to use these strategies now, the fact is, I'm a little worried. Rather than pick up one of those strategy cue cards, these kids could, instead, announce that they have no idea what they're supposed to do. They might even put their head on the table and shut down. Teachers have all seen this happen with kids at one time or another.

But, fortunately, I've never had this worst-case-scenario happen during any of my comprehension strategy practice sessions. And when the first child reaches for a cue-card, I realize that the children do understand what they're expected to do. And the rest of the kids in the group inevitably follow suit.

I'd like to think this successful release of responsibility from teacher to learner is testimony to the great teaching that preceded this moment. And maybe it is. But I think it's also possible that this exercise works as well as it generally does because children find this format for practicing reading strategies to be a lot of *fun*. I'm always curious to learn what the reading-strategy choices will reveal about the students' thinking. So I ask, "Who wants to share first?"

Makayla's hand shoots up. "I picked *Wondering* because I wonder if the kids will really get quiet after ten o'clock. I guess I'm *connecting*, too, because my friends and I never go to sleep that early when *I* have a party."

Then Renee adds, "I wondered the same thing as Makayla, but I am also *guessing* that they will stay up way past midnight, *and* they will get into lots of trouble."

Devon then *guesses* that they might get into trouble by breaking something valuable.

Robert *pictures* that this poem is about a boy.

Cherise says she is *picturing* a girl and can see her jumping up and down, begging her parents to allow her to have this party.

Willy then waves his *Noticing* card in the air. "I *noticed* that this kid got permission for this party from his dad, rather than from his mom. But I have to ask my mom when *I* want to invite kids over to the house."

I look at the *Noticing* card I am holding. I always wait until the end to share my thinking, in case a child has used the same strategy in a similar way. And it has happened again! "Willy and I noticed the exact same thing," I say. "When I was a kid, we had the same rules in our house: If I wanted to invite friends over, I had to check with Mom first."

Willy's grin lets me know he is surprised and rather pleased with himself for coming up with the same thought as the teacher. He sees first hand that his very own, unique point of view is valued. I am pleased to be part of Willy's self-validation, but I am not so surprised that we each used the same strategy in a similar way.

In traveling from classroom to classroom, sharing this approach to comprehension instruction, I have over the years, been pleased to discover that when you ask children what they are thinking, you find out—by golly, they really are thinking.

- **Repeat the reading-strategy-practice process through to completion of text selection.**
The group proceeds through the rest of the poem in this fashion; after we read a stanza together, we each pick up a cue-card to show the strategy that contributed most to our understanding. We share our thinking and maybe even laugh a little. Then we move on to the next block of text:

> *My friends came over to the house.*
> *They brought their sleeping stuff.*
> *We played full-contact football*
> *till it got a little rough.*

By this time in the practice session, students seldom need prodding from the teacher to choose a strategy cue-card. Instead, I generally enjoy my role as observer, watching students contemplate one reading strategy over another, finally making a decision.

There's a scramble this time for the *Picturing* cards, and Cherise looks disappointed when there isn't one left for her. "Is there another strategy that helped you?" I ask her. "I remember that you chose the *Picturing* card last time, too."

Cherise considers her options and then selects the *Connecting* cue card.

When a student repeatedly picks the same strategy cue-card, it may be because she has had success with that particular strategy and, therefore, feels safe using it again and again. But it's important that students get comfortable using several different strategies to understand what they read. To encourage students to practice using more strategies, the teacher can ask that everyone in the group pick up a different strategy cue-card after reading the next chunk of text.

I use two complete sets of strategy cards in this practice activity because it seems reasonable that more than one child may want to talk about a certain strategy after a text segment is read. If both the cue-cards for a particular strategy have already been scooped up, as in the example above, I ask the third student who wants to discuss that same strategy to, instead, think about a different strategy that was helpful in his understanding of the text segment. However, if a student seems to have an urgent wish to discuss a particular strategy following a text reading, and both cue-cards for that strategy are already in use, I may ask one of the children who is holding that card to simply pass it to her friend after she's shared, so the friend can then use it, too.

To avoid the issues that invariably arise over the supply and demand of strategy cue-cards in these small-group sessions, some teachers will want to give each student in the group a complete set of the cue-cards to use during the practice session. Then all of the students in the small group can choose from the full repertoire of comprehension strategies during each discussion period. But I recommend that you use no more than two sets of the cue cards for the entire group. The limited number of cue-cards available forces students to stretch their thinking beyond their first impulse.

I've also found that when the cue-cards are placed face-up on a table as the group moves through this strategy-practice activity, I can easily monitor which strategies are being used regularly and which are consistently left on the table. I may then make time in the practice session to model how to use the strategies that students are repeatedly overlooking in their choices for discussion.

If a student (or a group of students) consistently ignores one or more reading strategies, it's an important clue to the teacher to provide more targeted instruction in various applications of that particular strategy and to provide, as well, more opportunities for students to practice using that strategy. (You'll find many suggestions for targeted strategy lessons in Chapter Six and Seven. And, in Chapter Seven, I offer a detailed plan for incorporating strategy instruction into a comprehensive literacy curriculum.)

Don't be surprised when you begin these small-group practice sessions if your students miscall some strategies or use them somewhat inaccurately. If they used the strategies perfectly, they wouldn't need practice! One way to handle their misuse of a strategy is to suggest that a strategy a student identified as, for example, *noticing* is actually *figuring out*. And the teacher can model again for the students, as needed, the correct use of any of the strategies.

Students need to get comfortable using several different strategies to understand what they read.

- **As the practice session progresses, students will volunteer more readily to discuss their reading strategy choices.**
  In this example, as we moved stanza-by-stanza through the poem titled, "Sleepover," first reading and then sharing with the group the strategy we chose to understand each stanza, Devon held up one of the two *Picturing* cards and said, "I *picture* a lot of sleeping bags piled in a corner. Except, there are so many of them, they kind of overflow into the room."

  Renee, holding the other picturing card, added to Devon's picture. "In my mind," she said, "I see that some of the kids have brought along their teddy bears, too, and those are in the pile with the sleeping bags. And there are pillows."

  Robert, holding a *Noticing* card, was quick to tell us that he was certain he was right in his guess last time about the poem being about a boy. In this latest stanza, he *noticed* the line that read, "We played full-contact football."

  "Girls would *not* do that," he insisted.

  Cherise, however, voiced disagreement with Robert's discovery of textual evidence that supported his earlier *prediction* about who was hosting the slumber party. I told her that her different point of view was O.K., and I suggested to her and Robert that, in the stanzas that follow, the author may give us some more clues to help us figure out who is having this slumber party, a boy or a girl.

- **Find opportunities throughout the practice session to encourage students to return to the text to identify evidence that supports their point of view.**
  Because, in this example, Robert found additional clues in this latest stanza of the poem to support the *guess* he developed from what he *noticed* in the last stanza, I made a point to compliment him on his good reading-detective skills.

  "Robert," I said, "you found more evidence to support the guess you made last time about who is hosting this slumber party. Returning to the text for more clues, and more evidence to support your guesses, is exactly what good readers do!"

  Substantiating a point of view with proof from the text is a critical component of what students will in later grades refer to as "close reading." The practice of returning to the text to verify or discount speculations is a habit of mind that serves students well throughout their academic career and beyond. These skills are also critical to obtaining a satisfactory score on most state achievement tests.

So as students in the small-group practice sessions talk about the *pictures* they imagine when they read a text selection or when they describe something they've *figured out*, the teacher should, whenever possible, follow up with questions that bring their attention back to specific details in the text. You might ask, "Which lines in the poem helped you create that mental picture?" Or ask, "Which details in the text helped you reach your conclusion?"

The poem used in this example was short, and all of our reading and thinking and talking about our text in this practice session would probably be completed in about 20 minutes.

- **Once the entire text selection has been read and discussed, ask students to briefly summarize basic elements.**
  I ask the students to briefly summarize the basic story elements: characters, setting, the problem, a few events, and the resolution. And, usually, students can answer these questions easily by the conclusion of the session.

  Then I will inquire, "Why do you suppose it was so easy for you to come up with this summary?"

  The consensus is usually that stopping to think and talk about the thinking strategies we used made the text easy to understand — and easy to remember, too.

- **Ask students to reflect on their uses of reading strategies.**
  "Think about the strategies you've used today," I say. "Once you've decided on which strategy helped you most to understand the text, tell us where in the text that strategy was especially helpful for you."

  Sometimes I reflect orally with students about their strategy use; other times I give them an activity sheet for this purpose. Today I pass out the half-page "Strategy Slip" sheets (available for teachers on p. 156 and in the file titled, "ThreeB," on the CD). I model the way I would complete this form for my own reading of this text. Then I send the students back to their seats to complete the activity. They will return their completed slips to me at the conclusion of this morning's literacy block. Another useful activity sheet I often use as a strategy follow-up is the "Active Reader Report" found on page 155 and on the CD in the file titled, "ThreeB.")

- **Help students appreciate the skills they've begun to use in the practice session.**

  Before dismissing the students from this group, I tell them how proud I am of the great thinking they have just demonstrated, and I ask another question, "Do you think you are starting to understand these thinking strategies?" At this stage, students usually nod an enthusiastic response to this question. Then I ask another question. "Do you think you could use these strategies in your own reading?" This question generally brings more affirmative nods.

  Finally, I collect the strategy cue-cards. The students return to their desks with their copy of the poem we have just read, their "Strategy Slip," and, most importantly, a good feeling of accomplishment.

  I feel successful, too. I have brought these students to a place where they have begun to apply, in an integrated way, a repertoire of reading comprehension strategies, with which they can construct meaning from what they read. I have empowered them with a model for guided practice, a model that allows them to interact purposefully with the text before them, with their peers and with their teacher to understand what they read.

- **With repeated practice, students will gain proficiency in use of reading strategies.**

  As students gain proficiency in using these strategies during each guided-practice session, you will observe that they use the entire strategy repertoire appropriately. They find all the best clues in the text and do so without you prompting them. They also will begin to leave you out of their discussions as they share with each other their insights into text. Each sign of your diminishing role in these practice sessions is occasion for you to congratulate yourself; your students are gaining independence as able readers!

  In Chapter Eight you will find several rubrics to help you monitor and assess your students' application of these strategies, as well as their comprehension of text as a result of using these strategies. These rubrics will help you assess your students' strategic thinking abilities beyond only their oral use of strategies in these small-group practice sessions.

  Continue to celebrate your students' increasingly independent use of reading strategies by giving them longer segments of text to read before they are asked to stop to reflect. And give them the opportunity to conduct their discussions about reading without you present. While it would make little sense to leave a group of nonstrategic readers alone without a teacher to guide them, it makes perfect sense to do this with readers who have demonstrated their abilities to think strategically about text. But when students are working on their own in a small group, be sure that they are reading materials close to their independent reading level. Remember, *independent level* reading materials are texts that students can decode and comprehend easily by themselves, without guidance from a more knowledgeable reader (their teacher!). Even good readers, however, should continue to work with the teacher once or twice a week as they learn to strategically address more and more challenging texts.

Additional Strengths of this Strategy Practice Model Sustained over Time

At the outset of reading comprehension practice, young readers are a long way from using these strategies well by themselves. These are *not* the kinds of strategies your students can begin to practice on Monday and master by Friday. Rather, teachers should begin to engage students in practice using reading comprehension strategies in the students' primary grades and vigorously pursue their use of these strategies over several years. Your students' continued practice with these strategies will contribute to their achieving many important instructional and related social goals, including the following:

The practice of returning to the text to verify or discount speculation is a habit of mind that serves students well.

- **Listening Skills.**

  To participate meaningfully in a conversation, students must listen to what other members of their group say. When Tara announces that the question on her mind is the same as what Jack was wondering about, it's clear she was listening carefully to Jack. In order for Isabel to disagree with Charlie's text-to-text connection, she had to have heard the details he shared with the group. Good listeners can add to the discussion because they hear and remember their peer's contributions to the process of understanding text.

- **Oral Language Skills.**

  Many teachers report poor oral language skills among their students. Because this guided practice format generates a lot of student discussion, it offers teachers ample opportunity to encourage children to speak in complete sentences, to distinguish between language patterns appropriate for different audiences, and to help students expand their spoken vocabulary.

- **Sense of Camaraderie.**
  Much of students' time in the classroom is spent working individually, in a spirit of competition, rather than working collaboratively with their fellow students to achieve learning objectives. Some of that individual work is appropriate, of course. But it's good to balance students' individualism with curricula that encourages children to join forces to reach a common goal, in this case, a fuller understanding of a text they have read together. As students practice using comprehension strategies in small peer groups, they recognize that, by working together to understand the text, they will each achieve greater comprehension than any one of them could achieve alone. And the same kids who may have antagonized each other on the playground or in the lunchroom have the opportunity in these small-group practice sessions to discover that they have something in common, perhaps a similar connection to a piece of writing.

- **Encouragement for Struggling Readers.**
  Struggling readers thrive on blended-strategy practice because it keeps them actively engaged. They feel empowered by the invitation to construct meaning from text using strategies that *they* choose. With this practice technique, comprehension is not a matter of coming up with the "right" answers to the teacher's questions. So there is less risk of being "wrong." This model allows a struggling reader to have a voice in the conversation, a voice that is respected by the group. (Also see the section titled, "Modifications for Struggling Readers, Early Primary Readers, and Readers whose First Language Is Not English," beginning on page 59, later in this chapter.)

Following below is a quick teacher reference to implement the small-group, teacher-guided-practice model.

Nine Simple Steps to Practicing Comprehension Strategies

You will need:
- a short piece of text (one copy for each student)
- a large index card for each student
- two sets of strategy-cue cards (p. 245) or mini-posters (p. 226)
- a pad of small sticky notes

Step 1
Before you begin:
As a guide for the length of the text that will be discussed, use your sense of what the students can handle well in one session. Start with a reading that fits comfortably on a single sheet of paper or a couple of pages. Mark up your copy of the text to divide it into manageable chunks. As students become more competent with the use of strategies, work with larger chunks, from texts that extend over several pages, possibly a whole chapter.

Step 2
Read the text yourself, noting occasions when you used different comprehension strategies. If students miss key opportunities for using strategies during their own reading, you will be prepared to model or prompt good strategy use. Small sticky notes work well for making such notes on the text the small group will study, or you can make your notes in the margin.

Step 3
With your group:
When your group first convenes, review for the students the strategies that good readers use to comprehend text. Use the strategy cue-cards or mini-posters to make this task more concrete. This should only take a minute or two.

Step 4
Hand out the index cards and the reading selection and ask the students to cover up all but the first chunk of text.

Step 5

Ask the students to read the first chunk of text silently and be ready to tell you "what's going on in their head" related to their use of thinking strategies.

Step 6

Place the strategy cue cards on the table in front of the students and ask them to pick up the cue card with the strategy that has helped them most to comprehend the text they have just read. (If your students are grouped appropriately, there shouldn't be too many who lag far behind the others in reading rate.)

Step 7

Once all the students have finished reading the text chunk and selected a strategy cue-card, give each student a chance to share his/her strategy application. Encourage all students to participate. Monitor students' responses to check for understanding, misunderstanding, and opportunities to extend their thinking. As the students discuss the strategy they used, ask them to provide evidence for what they are saying by returning to the text for "proof." And note weaknesses in their use of any of these strategies so you can address those weaknesses when you provide explicit instruction in individual strategies later on.

Step 8

Repeat steps five through seven with subsequent chunks of text until the group has read the entire text and discussed the comprehension strategies they used in their reading.

Step 9

At the end of the group session, check students' understanding of what they've just read by asking a few basic questions about the text. Also ask students how their use of these six strategies improved their comprehension. Remember that your goal is to guide students toward independence; you want them to ultimately apply these strategies for reading comprehension whenever they read and without a teacher to guide them. So work systematically toward that goal.

Scheduling Comprehension Strategy Instruction

To help you bring your students to the point of independence, where they take charge of their own use of reading comprehension strategies, I have plotted for you, below, the gradual, step-by-step process I use to release to students responsibility for using these reading strategies.

The learning period that begins with the introduction of the strategies and extends to the point where students can discuss the strategies competently generally takes about 10 weeks. I phase-in strategy instruction over a five-day period, then consistently apply the model over the following nine weeks. Of course, this time-frame may vary based on the needs in your classroom.

When I first introduce comprehension strategies to students in the intermediate grades (generally grades three through six), my initial week of instruction looks something like this:

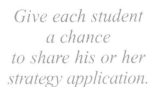

Give each student a chance to share his or her strategy application.

Week One

Monday

1. **Whole-class overview/explanation** of all six strategies (about 15 minutes)

2. **Whole-class teacher modeling** of use of integrated strategies in a Read-Aloud/Think-Aloud session, using a picture book (about 20 minutes)

3. **Small-group, teacher-guided student practice** of integrated use of reading strategies, focusing on a short text appropriate to students' instructional reading level (about 20 minutes) while the rest of the class is engaged with other literacy work.

4. **Whole-class reflection** on use of strategies for improved comprehension (5-10 minutes)

Tuesday

1. **Whole-class review** of strategy definitions and discussion of how each strategy is important to reading comprehension (about 10 minutes)

2. **Whole-class teacher modeling** of integrated strategy use in a Read-Aloud/Think-Aloud session, using a picture book (about 20 minutes). Students should begin to think aloud with the teacher about *their* applications of different strategies.

3. **Small-group, teacher-guided student practice** of integrated use of reading strategies, focusing on a short text appropriate to students' instructional reading level (about 20 minutes) while the rest of the class is engaged with other literacy work. (Different small group than teacher worked with on Monday.)

4. **Whole-class reflection** on use of strategies for improved comprehension (5-10 minutes)

Wednesday through Friday

1. **Whole-class review** of strategy definitions and how each strategy is important to reading comprehension (about 5-10 minutes)

2. **Whole-class teacher modeling** of integrated strategies with a Read-Aloud/Think-Aloud session, using a picture book (about 20 minutes). Students should assume increasing responsibility for thinking aloud about *their* application of different strategies, with prompting by the teacher as necessary.

3. **Small-group, teacher-guided student practice** of integrated use of reading strategies, focusing on a short text appropriate to students' instructional-reading level (about 20 minutes) while the rest of the class is engaged with other literacy work. (By the end of this first week, all small groups should have had at least one opportunity to meet with the teacher for guided practice using comprehension strategies.)

4. **Whole-class reflection** on use of strategies for improved comprehension (about 5-10 minutes)

Weeks Two through 10 (approximately)

Monday through Friday

1. **Brief review** of names and definitions of comprehension strategies and relevance of each strategy to reading comprehension (about 5 minutes)

2. **Whole-class teacher modeling** of use of integrated strategies with a Read-Aloud/Think-Aloud session, using a picture book or other short text. This teacher modeling should occur approximately 2-3 times per week, with each modeling session lasting about 20 minutes. The teacher should notice which strategies students use well and which they do not use as competently.

3. **Small-group student practice** with integrated comprehension strategies with two or more groups of readers using selections of short text at their instructional reading levels (about 20 minutes per group while the rest of the class is engaged in other literacy-related work, which may include comprehension strategy follow-up activities that have been gradually introduced and modeled.)

4. By about the second week of strategy practice, students are usually ready to **reflect in writing about their use of reading comprehension strategies**. I often begin with the "Strategy Slip" (page 156), as it is the simplest writing assignment for students to use. The "Active Reader Report" (on page 155) is great for older students or more competent readers. When I first introduce (and model) this follow-up activity, I ask students to complete it *after* we have read and discussed a selection of short text together. But as students become more familiar with the strategies and the "Active Reader Report," I sometimes request that they read a short text and complete this sheet *before* their small group convenes to discuss the same text. The students' written responses in the "Active Reader Report" then launch our small-group discussion of the text.

5. The literacy block should always end with **whole-class reflection** on the usefulness of these strategies to enhance reading comprehension (about 10 minutes).

After about 10 weeks of this routine
Teachers should at this point have a good sense of which strategies are easiest for which students to use and any problems students may be having as they apply the strategies to understand character, plot, details of informational text, or other dimensions of literature, whether fiction or nonfiction. As we gain a better perception of our students' comprehension strategy strengths and remaining needs for instruction, we can fine-tune our instruction.

Now it's time to use these strategies, not just to teach the *reader*, but also to teach the *reading*; the second part of this book, Embedding Reading Comprehension Strategies during Shared, Guided and Independent Reading, will detail how to teach more advanced uses of reading comprehension strategies.

But for struggling or younger readers, let's first explore some alternative ways teachers can best release to these students responsibility for their comprehension strategy learning.

Modifications for Struggling Readers, Early Primary Readers, and Readers whose First Language Is Not English

The initial introduction of blended strategies may differ for struggling readers, for early primary readers, and for readers whose first language is not English. I know from my own experiences teaching and from what I have heard over the years from many other teachers, too, that most students do just fine when *all* of the six comprehension strategies are introduced together. However, a more gradual introduction to these strategies is also possible, and this approach may be better for more challenged readers.

For these students, I suggest a start-up plan that begins with an introduction of just two strategies, *connecting* and *picturing*. Students generally regard these strategies as the most concrete, and that makes them a good place to start. I offer them more than just one comprehension strategy, right from the start, so that they have options in applying the strategies. Perhaps a student cannot *connect* to a particular text from her own experiences, but the text may have allowed her to *picture* something vividly in her mind.

After introducing these two strategies in one session, I will then, by about the third week, introduce the comprehension strategies, *Wondering* and *Guessing,* pointing out how questions often lead to predictions or hypotheses. I will work on these two strategies with them for the next couple of weeks. In whole-class modeling sessions and small-group practice sessions, add these two new strategies to the first two strategies you introduced before. These students can now practice in small groups integrated use of a repertoire of four possible comprehension strategies.

Finally, I introduce the strategies, *Noticing* and *Figuring Out*. These two comprehension strategies are also logically paired together because for a reader to *figure out (infer* or *synthesize)*, he must *notice* the details the author has provided. To draw a conclusion or integrate the text elements into a connected whole, the reader must notice the details the author has chosen to write. After working on these last two strategies for a short time, perhaps another two weeks, these strategies can be added to the rest of the strategy package. From that point forward, students can draw upon all six thinking strategies as they read, whether in teacher-guided small groups or independently.

A more gradual introduction to reading strategy may be better for more challenged readers.

This plan of introducing the six comprehension strategies in small portions, two-at-a-time, requires approximately two months and might unfold in your classroom like this:

Weeks One and Two

On the first day, introduce and explain the *Connecting* and *Picturing* strategy pair in language that is clear and simple enough for these more challenged students. After the first day, be sure to review the basic definitions at the beginning of every lesson. It is also helpful to use the mini-posters with the graphic icons during your introductions.

Subsequently model *Connecting* and *Picturing* for your students. Model the integrated use of these comprehension strategies a few times each week in a whole class Read-Aloud/Think Aloud session using picture books. After your students have watched and listened to your modeling of these first two strategies for a few sessions, encourage them to think along with you about their use of these strategies and to verbalize examples of their use of these strategies. Conclude each modeling session with a discussion of how comprehension strategies help us to become good readers.

If your students are not yet reading, their practice using these strategies in small groups must begin with you reading the text to them. The students can then use the strategy cue-cards to identify and talk about their comprehension-strategy choice after you have read each chunk of text out loud. (Even students who cannot read enjoy using these cue-cards to demonstrate and discuss the strategies they use to understand text that is read to them.)

If your students *are* ready for reading in these small-group practice sessions, be careful to choose texts that match their reading abilities. Many of the early guided-reading books won't have much content to un-package in a demonstration of reading comprehension strategies. But nonfiction selections offer some potential for demonstrating these strategies.

Weeks Three and Four
Continue the same format as above, focusing on *Wondering* and *Guessing*.

Weeks Five and Six
Continue the same format as above now incorporating a total of four strategies: *Connecting, Picturing, Wondering,* and *Guessing.*

Weeks Seven and Eight
Continue the same format as above with *Noticing* and *Figuring Out.*

After about Eight or Ten weeks
Continue the same format as above with all six comprehension strategies: *Connecting, Picturing, Wondering, Guessing, Noticing,* and *Figuring Out.*

4

Getting Past Mediocre Strategy Instruction

To recognize the difference between superficial and substantial comprehension-strategy instruction, keep in mind the following criteria that identify quality strategy instruction:

Teachers need to:

- Recognize when students need more intensive work on individual strategies to enhance their understanding of fiction and informational text;

- Explain specific reading comprehension strategies in a way that is meaningful for students considering the students' grade level;

- Model use of a comprehension strategy extensively, so students can see first-hand what that strategy looks like in action and how the strategy works together with other strategies to expand their understanding of text;

- Allow students ample opportunities for guided practice using the target strategy within a blended repertoire of comprehension strategies with text that is appropriate to the students' *instructional* level;

- Allow students to *apply* the target strategy within a blended repertoire of comprehension strategies with text that is appropriate to the students' *independent* level;

- Provide opportunities for students to reflect on their use of the specific strategy to enhance their understanding of the reading process as well as their understanding of themselves as readers.

Guiding Students to Proficiency with Reading Strategies

Powerful teaching (and better learning!) happens when a teacher understands the essential ingredients of shared, guided and independent reading and the role of these components within the comprehensive literacy framework. Providing students with an effective introduction to the strategies is essential. Beyond the introduction, however, instruction in use of a single strategy should always focus on a *specific application* of that strategy, rather than on a broad strategy *concept.*

To demonstrate the difference between mediocre and excellent comprehension instruction, consider the following example from a second-grade classroom. This classroom looks inviting, with spaces for children to work alone or as a large group. There's a cozy book-nook where kids can read; it has beanbag chairs, an area rug, shelves of stories attractively arranged at the students' eye level, and even a table lamp for extra ambience. The bulletin boards contain examples of students' work, authentic reading-writing tasks — none of those teacher-store cardboard cutouts here.

About twenty-five children are gathered on the rug in the meeting area. A teacher is seated on a chair, facing them. A picture book lies on her lap as she quietly asks for everyone's attention. And she doesn't have to ask twice.

"Today I'm going to read you a story," she begins. (It's a fairytale, although not one I recognize.) "I'm going to show you how good readers ask questions as they read," she says. "I will stop at different points in this story and think out loud about the questions I am wondering about as I read. Is everyone ready now to be a good listener?"

They are. And the teacher does exactly as she promised; she reads a page or two and then pauses to share with her students the question inspired by that segment of text: "Here's a place where I have a question," she reflects. "I'm wondering what the little old lady will do next?" She reads another page, stops to share another wondering question, then reads a bit more, stops to share yet another question. And so it goes.

Children begin to raise their hands now, eager to contribute their own thinking. From the front row, a cutie with braids says, "I have a question." But the teacher stops her. "No, no," she says. "It's my turn to be a good thinker; you'll have your turn in a few minutes. Right now,

Your strategy instruction should always focus on a specific application of a strategy.

your job is to be a good listener." And then the teacher returns to her reading and resumes thinking aloud about questions inspired by the text.

But no answers follow her questions, simply more questions. By the end of the story, however, the teacher notes that she has, in fact, discovered the answers to several of her questions. By this time, the group of second-graders has been sitting quietly (if not completely attentively) for about fifteen minutes, and the teacher recognizes that it's a good time to change the format to allow for their participation.

"Here's what we're going to do," she announces. "We're going to read in pairs. I've already made up the pairs and selected a book for you to read with your partner. I'm going to give you some sticky notes. I want you to stop while you're reading, whenever a question pops into your mind, and jot your question on the sticky note. Place the note on the page where you began to ask the question."

In a mostly-orderly manner, pairs of children and books march off to various classroom corners to do their reading. I wait and watch for a moment or two, then I shoe-horn my way into a tight space behind a bookcase, where two little boys are reading *Twinnies*, a picture book by Eve Bunting.

The first reader begins, "Last June I got twin baby sitters [sisters]. The w-wuh-wuh-where.....what's that word?" he inquires.

"Worst," I offer, sweeping my finger across the word from left to right hoping my new friend will focus on the visual cues.

"The worst that [thing] is that three [there] are two of them."

Then the first reader moves the book closer to his partner so he can have a go at the next page. The partner, preoccupied with distractions from elsewhere in the room, focuses his gaze toward the book, but stumbles through the first sentence and then declares, "You read it; I don't know the words."

Child One doesn't miss a beat although he does miss several words on the next page or two. I am tempted to intercede and remind the boys that they are overlooking the primary goal of the activity: to note questions that occur to them as they read and record them on the sticky notes. But I restrain myself, wondering if and when the boys will turn their attention to this task.

And then they do. I can't quite figure out their rationale for halting when they do. But one reader suddenly declares, "We need to ask a question!"

Both boys study the page in front of them. "Why is the girl holding the baby's hand?" This question, I expect, is derived from the illustration in the book as there is no mention of hand-holding in the text. (Reading the text, however, may have offered an answer to this question.) After a number of erasures, the question is neatly (if not accurately) penned on the note and affixed to the page. I think a couple of additional questions, also fairly obscure details, receive mention before the teacher calls the group back to the meeting area.

By then, I have moved on to another partnership, two girls who are engrossed in one of the Amelia Bedelia ("Emily Bed-a-whatever") stories through which they demonstrate similar strategy application.

Later, back on the rug in the meeting area, children are eager to share the questions they have created. The two boys' "hand-holding" inquiry seems as appropriate as others described and receives hearty approval from the teacher. She congratulates all the children for their use of "good reader" strategies. And the lesson concludes.

Successful Teaching Methods Help Children to Use Reading Strategies Most Effectively

Apply the following questions to consider what worked in the teaching/learning scenario above and what didn't work. Find evidence from the scenario to support your answers.

What did you think about the learning community? How would you rate the classroom environment? What about the rapport between the teacher and the students?

What did you think about the text used for modeling? Did the text seem appropriate and well-matched to this particular strategy? Was it matched to the interests of the students?

Did the teacher explain the strategy clearly? Was the lesson focused specifically enough? What information did she offer students in her explanation of the strategy they were studying?

What did you think about the teacher's modeling? Did the teacher do enough modeling? How did the teacher involve the students in that part of the lesson?

What did you think about the way the teacher provided for guided practice? Was the size of the small groups appropriate? Did students apply the targeted strategy (and other strategies) accurately? Did reflecting on strategies seem to contribute to the students' comprehension of what they read? To what extent were all students engaged in the conversation about the text?

What did you think about the way the teacher provided for application of the strategy? Did students appear to be reading from texts at their independent reading level? Were students self-directed in completing follow-up strategy applications? Why or why not?

How effective was the reflection? Did closure of the session include students' reflection on their use of the strategy? Did the reflection seem to reinforce students' understanding of the reading process?

Assuming you've now reflected on these considerations, let's compare our impressions. First, there were a number of positive things in this scenario. The classroom environment clearly supported the kind of literacy opportunities we wish for all of our students. There were a lot of books, which were well organized, easily accessible and attractively displayed. There were areas for the whole class to come together to work, spaces for small-group interaction, and cozy places for individual students to curl up with a good book, too. A feeling of mutual respect characterized the interaction among the students and between the students and the teacher. This classroom is a happy place to learn.

With regard to the lesson itself, it appears that the teacher felt that her students would benefit from an intensive lesson with one of the strategies: *Questioning* (or *Wondering*). She set about to provide that instruction. She chose a picture book suitable to students at her grade level, and she was careful as she read to pause following text segments of a reasonable length to model the questions that occurred to her as she read. In my opinion, she got some of the basics right, but she missed many of the fine points that could have made her teaching more effective.

First, focusing on an entire strategy (*Wondering, Picturing*, etc.) is too broad for one lesson. A more meaningful approach is to teach *one particular application* of the strategy, based on the text in the book you've selected for modeling a strategy for your class. In this case, the teacher could have zeroed in on *wondering* why the little old lady behaved in a certain way, focusing her use of the strategy *wondering* on character development. Or the teacher might have *wondered* what would happen next in the story, focusing her application of the strategy of *wondering* on the plot. Targeting her lesson to a specific application of a strategy would have made the lesson more accessible for her students and allowed the teacher to use all of the dimensions of explicit instruction.

To be effective, explicit instruction must begin with a good explanation of the reading comprehension strategy you intend to teach. First define the strategy for your students, and then let them know some of the ways that effective readers use the strategy, examples of when and how the strategy aids reading comprehension.

In the classroom presented in this example, the teacher omitted any kind of explanation of the strategy she intended to model. Instead, she jumped right into the modeling. But kids don't generally put these pieces together without explicit guidance. They might listen attentively and politely as their teacher describes her thinking about the book she is reading to them. But they are not likely to understand why she is sharing her thoughts with them unless she has, before beginning to model a reading strategy, explained to her students, in terms they can easily understand, the strategy she will use to understand the text she reads.

Without the context such an explanation provides, children are unlikely to transfer the example of her modeling to their own comprehension process as they read. The absence of any explanation from the teacher concerning the strategy she used in her modeling probably explains why these second graders seemed mystified as they attempted to derive their own questions from the books they were reading.

The best modeling gradually releases some of the responsibility for the task from teacher to learners. As students participate, even in limited

To teach students to think strategically a teacher must make the strategy explicit.

ways, the teacher can estimate the extent to which they "get it." She can begin to assess from their suggestions and responses whether they understand the process well enough to apply it more independently. But because this teacher emphatically resisted her students' overtures to contribute during the modeling phase of the lesson, by the time she reached the end of the text, she still had no information about how much of her lesson her students understood.

When a teacher sets her students free to apply new knowledge, but she has little or no awareness of their level of competence with the new skills she has presented to them, she takes a chance on losing the value of her lesson. And in the example above, the teacher gambled and lost.

Her students understood the mechanics of their assignment: writing questions about the text onto sticky notes and affixing those notes to the pages in the book where those questions arose for them. But the teacher had not equipped them with any plan they could use to focus their questions, to most usefully apply the *wondering* strategy while they read. And that's why so many of the questions her students came up with were substandard. In order to teach students to think strategically, a teacher must make the strategy explicit.

Compounding the problems in this example, the teacher entirely omitted the guided-practice phase of instruction and moved directly to an independent application of the strategy. Additionally, some of the texts she assigned appeared to be above the independent reading level of her students. As a result, the level of frustration some of her young readers experienced as they struggled to read the text distracted them from their use of the reading comprehension strategy, *Wondering*.

The teacher did pull the class together at the end of the lesson to reflect on what they had learned (an important final step of good instruction). But all responses, even the marginally appropriate questions, were equally celebrated. While we don't want to demean students for missing the mark, neither do we want to allow them to continue thinking that mediocrity is the same as excellence. It isn't. The teacher in this example missed an opportunity to show her students the difference between an effective question, which probes the main idea in a text, and an extraneous question, which may concern only a minor detail in the story. She could have identified for her class what she liked about a particularly good question. "Did you all hear Javon's question?" she might have said.

"He asked, 'I wonder if Little Red Riding Hood will ever talk to strangers again?' Now I love *that* question," she could have crowed. "That kind of question helps us think about a really important idea from that story. What's the idea?"

An enthusiastic response from a teacher, focusing the children's attention on a particularly valuable question, can empower all the students in the class to understand the value of a very effective use of a strategy over a mediocre application of it. A more targeted emphasis on the strategy, in this example, *wondering*, would have also helped the teacher to monitor students' proficiency with that strategy.

Moving Forward with Comprehension Strategy Instruction

With a little guidance, I think this second grade teacher could have transformed her lesson from average to awesome. She could have focused the instruction more precisely on one particular application of the *questioning* strategy, and taught this explicitly through the contexts of both shared and guided reading.

The remainder of this book offers the kind of support that could have helped this second grade teacher. And it can help other teachers, too. It includes over one hundred strategy applications for both fiction and informational text. It provides a framework for incorporating comprehension strategies into a comprehensive literacy curriculum of shared, guided, and independent reading. And it offers some suggestions for monitoring and assessing how well students understand and use comprehension strategies.

Remember, even as we teach lessons on specific strategy applications, that the ultimate goal of all work with comprehension strategies is to *blend those small pieces back into the whole strategy package.*
If you teach with that intention, your students' use of reading comprehension strategies (and their comprehension) will spiral upward toward proficiency.

Embedding Comprehension Strategies During Shared, Guided, and Independent Reading

5

Applying Comprehension Strategies
to Study Fiction

 Comprehension-strategy instruction helps students learn to analyze fiction.

 Comprehension strategies help students understand literary elements — characterization, plot, setting, problem and author's craft.

 Teaching comprehension strategies with specific application to such elements is more effective than teaching a strategy more generally, as a concept, without specific application.

 Theme, author, and genre studies provide the framework for a year-long literacy curriculum with a focus on reading comprehension strategies.

Studying Literature Strategically

There was a time when analyzing a work of literature was something children were taught to do in high school. I remember, somewhere around the ninth grade, hearing my English teacher ask our class, "What do you think made Ethan Frome behave the way he did?"

And I thought to myself, "What does his motivation matter? Let's just get on with the reading and find out how the story ends!"

Although I have always loved reading and in high school considered myself to be "a good reader," until that moment in ninth grade, I believed that good reading was synonymous with comprehending plot.

These days we introduce students to the idea of literary analysis at a much earlier age — during kindergarten. We know that, with careful instruction, even young children are capable of digging deeper into their literature. Additionally, children benefit most from these strategies when they learn to apply them to increase their understanding of literature.

Reading comprehension strategies can — and should — be applied to the investigation of literary elements: character development, plot, setting, problem, and author's craft. Strategies for reading comprehension should be a natural part of studying literature, and the teaching of these strategies should be a central focus of your students' literature studies.

Begin by teaching a focused lesson on particular applications of a strategy, rather than addressing a strategy concept globally. We can teach *many* focused lessons on applications of each and all of the strategies. Over time, this method will strengthen students' ability to understand great authors and great works of literature — whether Dr. Seuss or *Dr. Zhivago!*

The charts on pages 79 through 83 identify focus points for lessons that apply reading comprehension strategies to the study of literature. Each bulleted item in these charts is designed to be the focus of a lesson or short series of lessons. You'll find charts for lessons on Character Development, Setting, Problem/Conflict, Plot/Events, and Author's Craft. (These charts are also included on the CD in file titled, "Five.") Sample lesson plans and templates are in Chapter 7, "Teaching Comprehension Strategies in Shared, Guided and Independent Reading."

Creating a Year-long Literacy Curriculum to Study Theme, Genre, and Author through Applied Use of Reading Comprehension Strategies

Teaching specific applications of reading comprehension strategies will help your students to become effective readers. But the approach becomes even more powerful when we teach these strategies as the core of a thoughtfully designed, full-year curriculum of literature studies.

To systematically incorporate your instruction in reading comprehension strategies into literature studies, you will need to take a longer view of your instruction. Rather than randomly choosing works of literature for study in September and other, unrelated literature in October, divide the academic year among theme, genre, and author studies. That way, students get to study each text in a broader context.

One way to approach literature is through themes. And themes can be as varied as our imagination permits. Here are some of my favorites:

Themes for Study

Defining "family"	Consider the environment
Uncommon courage of common people	Siblings and other rivals
Turning points	Making the right decision
Finding what matters most	Home is where the heart is
Winning against the odds	What's real?
Learning life's little lessons	Follow your dreams
We all have a right to belong	Learning lasts a lifetime
Surviving nature	Living by wise words
War brings death and destruction	Symbols of hope
Discrimination hurts	Alternative points of view
People with special passions	Girl power

Listing books under each thematic heading would be as extensive as the list of themes itself. Of course, many books could address a variety of themes. And some are more appropriate for younger readers while others are better suited for older students.

Theme offers one useful way to organize literature study. But it certainly is not the only way. You also can organize literacy learning around the study of different genres and sub-genres within each broad category. Remember that each genre can be "packaged" through a variety of literary formats. Here are some genres and a sampling of common literary formats:

Genres for Study

Realistic fiction	Fantasy
Mystery	Science fiction
Traditional fairytales	Biography
Fables	Modernized folk tales
Myths and legends	Historical fiction
Tall tales	Narrative nonfiction
Multicultural folk tales	Memoir

Literary Formats

Novels	Plays
Short stories	Journals
Poetry	Letters
Picture books	News article

Investigating individual authors is another way to organize literature study. But how could we possibly narrow that list to fewer than several dozens of names? Impossible! However, you can make author studies especially rich by selecting authors who have written in two or three different literary formats, such as novels, short stories, picture books, etc. At the risk of overlooking too many of my favorite authors, here are just a few too-good-to-miss names to keep in mind:

My Favorite Authors for Author Studies

Avi	Robert Munsch
Judy Blume	Patricia MacLachlan
Jan Brett	Patricia McKissack
Eve Bunting	Barbara Park
Lynne Cherry	Katherine Patterson
Beverly Cleary	Gary Paulsen
Andrew Clement	Patricia Polacco
Tomie dePaola	Faith Ringgold
Mem Fox	Cynthia Rylant
Jean Craighead George	Allen Say
Kevin Henkes	John Scieszka
Karen Hesse	Dr. Seuss
Sara Holbrook	Shel Silverstein
Ezra Jack Keats	Jerry Spinelli
Karla Kuskin	Mark Teague
Kathryn Lasky	Chris Van Allsburg
Thomas Locker	Jane Yolen

Teach these strategies as the core of a full-year curriculum of literature studies.

We could probably keep kids reading for their entire school career through author studies alone. But we really should integrate our literature curriculum with study of theme and genre. And be sure to include nonfiction in your year-long comprehensive literacy curriculum. (See Chapter Six for more specific ideas for teaching reading comprehension strategies using informational text.)

The chart below provides a complete sample curricular plan that will help your students truly *study* literature as they learn to use reading comprehension strategies effectively. Use any of the specific strategy applications mentioned in the chart as the focal point of a shared-reading lesson. That strategy can then be integrated into the strategy repertoire, practiced during guided reading, and applied through independent reading. A similar instructional sequence could be followed for strategy applications with nonfiction texts.

We can put these elements together to build a year-long literacy curriculum at the intermediate grade level, incorporating study of author, theme, and genre and focusing concurrently on application of reading comprehension strategies. The following full-year sample literacy plan meets *all* of those criteria.

Sample Year-Long Literacy Curriculum For an Intermediate Grade

First six weeks	• Review of integrated comprehension-strategy model with a variety of short text
Next four weeks	• Theme study. Siblings and other rivals, emphasizing the application of comprehension strategies to characterization and plot
Next four weeks	• Genre study. Multi-cultural folk tales, emphasizing application of comprehension strategies to conflict/problem/theme and setting
Next four weeks	• Single-author study. Patricia Polacco, emphasizing application of comprehension strategies to author's craft
Next four weeks	• Single-author study. Chris Van Allsburg, emphasizing the application of comprehension strategies to author's craft
Next four weeks	• Theme study. Home Is Where the Heart Is, emphasizing the application of comprehension strategies to setting and characterization
Next four weeks	• Study of expository text, emphasizing application of comprehension strategies to informational text (See Chapter Seven)
Next four weeks	• Genre study. Mystery, emphasizing the application of comprehension strategies to setting and plot
Next four weeks	• School-wide theme study. Winning in spite of the odds, emphasizing the application of comprehension strategies to characterization and conflict/problem/theme

Any part of this example could be changed to fit your needs, of course, including varying the sequence of instruction or the number of weeks for each study and substituting other themes, authors and genres to satisfy standards, curriculum, or testing requirements. But in any study plan, several literary elements should ultimately be included, although the targeted literary elements might change.

The number of weeks spent on the initial teaching or review of the basic comprehension strategy model will depend upon the grade level and the extent of your students' prior knowledge about comprehension strategies. Students in the lower grades (second and third) will most likely work with just the "generic" model for much of the year. But upper-elementary grade and middle school teachers and students will want to make the transition to the literature-based model as efficiently as possible.

It is critical, however, to incorporate multiple dimensions of fiction (character development, setting, problem/conflict, etc.) into a year-long plan. Without such planning, the result is often a lopsided curriculum that may focus heavily on plot or some other literary element, but neglect any substantial work in another area, such as author's craft. For the same reason, it's also helpful to map out how and when you will address author, genre, and theme studies.

Some teachers ask if a scope and sequence should be developed for teaching strategy focus lessons. I am wary of rigid scope and sequence charts. While it is important to teach *explicitly*, developing any lock-step sequential plan tends to make teaching far too *prescriptive*. If we are sincere about wanting to meet the *real* needs of the readers in our classroom, we will listen carefully as they talk about text and chart the course of our comprehension curriculum accordingly.

Teachers also wonder how long they should spend on one individual focus lesson. The answer to this question will become clearer in Chapter Seven, but remember that a "lesson" needn't be completed in a single session. Also keep in mind that you can revisit the same strategy application more than once during a year, and over many years, allowing students to explore the same application many times. Similarly, the same text can be used for more than one strategy focus.

Finally, keep in mind that this is *not* a complete list of strategy applications. There are plenty of applications here to get you started, but other possibilities can certainly be imagined and implemented by teachers. What do your students need to know about reading literature in order to improve their comprehension? Transform that need into one of the reading comprehension strategies. Then add that application to one of the charts in this chapter — or maybe you'll want to design a whole new chart with a different focus.

Before considering, in Chapter Seven, how *all* of these instructional components will come together in the classroom through shared, guided, and independent reading, the next chapter will help you to explore the role informational text can play in this curriculum.

Studying Literature Strategically:
Focusing on Character Development

Strategy	Possible Focus Lessons
Connecting	• Find ways that a character in this story reminds me of myself. • Find ways that a character in this story reminds me of a character in other books I have read. • Find ways that a character in this story reminds me of a real person in our world today or someone famous who may have lived a long time ago.
Picturing	• Picture the way a character looks. (Use my imagination as well as the words on the page.)
Wondering	• Wonder about why a character behaves in a certain way. (What makes a character do and say certain things?) • Wonder why the author included a particular character.
Predicting/Guessing	• Based on things I know about this character already, predict how that character will react to a situation, event, or problem in the story.
Noticing	• Notice what a character does or says or thinks to provide clues to what is important to him or her. • Notice the actions, motives, and feelings of a character. • Notice what the author did to make a character seem believable. • Notice which characters are primary (or main characters) and which characters are secondary characters. (How are these characters different?)
Figuring Out (Synthesizing or Inferring)	• Figure out how one of the characters is important to the story. • Choose one word that best describes a particular character and explain why this word fits this character. • Figure out how a particular character contributed to the solution of the problem in the story. • Figure out how a particular character changed from the beginning to the end of the story. • Figure out what was important to a particular character; tell how I know that from the story. • Figure out how the story might have been different if a particular character behaved in a different way. • Figure out whether I would have behaved in the same way as a particular character behaved in the story. What might I have done differently? • Figure out whether a particular character shaped the events in the story or whether the events shaped the character.

Studying Literature Strategically: Focusing on Setting

Strategy	Possible Focus Lessons
Connecting	• Determine how this place reminds me of somewhere I know. • Consider how this place is similar to or different from a place I have been. • Decide whether I would like to go to visit or live in this place. Tell why I would or would not want to visit or live there.
Picturing	• Picture this place, including the small details. • Use all of my senses to get an even stronger picture of this place.
Wondering	• Wonder how the setting (the time and place) will be important to this story. • Wonder whether the story would be different if it took place somewhere else, or during another time. • Wonder why the author chose this particular setting (time and place) for this story.
Predicting/Guessing	• Predict how the characters will use the setting to their advantage to solve their problem or how the setting will make it difficult for them to solve the problem.
Noticing	• Notice when the setting changes in the story. • Notice how the author makes the setting seem believable. • Notice whether the setting is an integral part of the story or if the story could have taken place anywhere.
Figuring Out (Synthesizing or Inferring)	• Figure out how the story would have been different if it occurred somewhere else, or in another time. • Figure out how the setting was important to what happened in the story.

Studying Literature Strategically:
Focusing on Problem/Conflict

Strategy	Possible Focus Lessons
Connecting	• Consider how the problem in this story is similar to a problem I have had in my own life. • Consider how the problem in this story is similar to the problem in another story I read. • Consider how the problem in this story reminds me of a problem faced by people in our world today.
Picturing	• Make a picture in my mind of the problem as it unfolds in the story. (How many senses can I use to get a really good picture of this problem in my mind?)
Wondering	• Determine how this problem will probably be solved.
Predicting/Guessing	• Predict the outcome of the problem based on what I know about the characters and other things in the story.
Noticing	• Notice details that contribute to the problem or to the solution of the problem. • Notice the kind of conflict. (Character vs. character? Character vs. nature? Character vs. society? Character vs. self?)
Figuring Out (Synthesizing or Inferring)	• Figure out how I would have solved this problem if it had been my problem. • Figure out what the author wants me to learn from the problem in this story.

Studying Literature Strategically: Focusing on Plot/Events

Strategy	Possible Focus Lessons
Connecting	• Connect events in the story to similar things that have happened to me in my own life. • Connect events in the story to similar events in other stories. • Connect events in the story to situations in the world today or in the past.
Picturing	• Picture the events in the story as they occur. (Can I use all of my senses to get a really clear image of these events?)
Wondering	• Wonder what will happen next. • Wonder why the author included a particular detail or particular information.
Predicting/Guessing	• Predict the next event. • Predict the outcome of the story.
Noticing	• Notice the clues that the author provides to let me know what is going to happen next. • Notice how the author builds suspense. • Notice what seems real and what could never happen. • Notice the plot structure. (Is it episodic or progressive, or are there parallel plots that build simultaneously?)
Figuring Out (Synthesizing or Inferring)	• Figure out how all the story parts -- characters, setting, and events -- come together in the end to solve the problem. • Figure out which clues were the most useful in understanding this story. • Figure out what might happen next if this story were to be continued.

Studying Literature Strategically: Focusing on Author's Craft

Strategy	Possible Focus Lessons
Connecting	• Consider what I know about the genre the author has chosen and the special characteristics of this genre. • Consider other things I've read by the same author. (How do those texts help me know what to expect from this text?)
Picturing	• Picture the characters, the events, the setting. (How does the author make these believable?) • Determine how the illustrations enhance the text? • Determine whether the style of the illustrations seems well-matched to the style of the writing?
Wondering	• Wonder why the author chose this genre or structure to tell this story. • Wonder why the author chose this title. • Wonder why the author chose this illustrator.
Predicting/Guessing	• Predict the events that may happen in this story or the outcome of this story based on what I know about this genre or author.
Noticing	• Notice who is narrating the story. (Why did the author choose this voice?) • Notice how the author develops the story. (Can I find all the story elements — characters, setting, problem, events, solution, ending?) • Notice whether the story is told from one point of view or more than one point of view. (What does each voice contribute to the story?) • Notice how the plot is laid out. (Does one event follow another, or are there flash backs, or more than one story occurring at the same time?) • Notice the way the story begins and ends. (How does the author get my attention? Is the ending a satisfying one? Why?) • Notice the things that the author does to make me react to the story in a particular way. (How does the author make the story funny, sad, suspenseful, adventurous, etc.?) • Notice the tone of the author's voice. (Is it formal or informal? How does the voice make a difference to the story?) • Notice the little tricks the author uses to make the sentences flow smoothly. (Can I find some examples of craft at work?) • Notice the words the author uses. (Are they precise and powerful?)
Figuring Out (Synthesizing or Inferring)	• Figure out whether I think this is good literature. (Why do I think this is, or is not, good literature?) • Figure out how this story might be different if the author used another genre, another voice, or wrote it for readers of a different age level. • Figure out how this story might have been different if it was written by another author.

6

Applying Comprehension Strategies in the Content Areas

⚙ The same comprehension strategies are useful for both fiction and nonfiction, although they are applied a little differently.

⚙ We can teach comprehension strategies in an integrated way to meet the additional demands of content area *texts*.

⚙ Using an integrated approach to comprehension strategies *before* reading informational text can help to prepare students for the reading ahead.

⚙ Blending comprehension strategies *during* and *after* reading informational text helps students construct basic meaning and think critically about content-area knowledge.

⚙ Focused lessons fine-tune the ability of students to use comprehension strategies as a reading tool.

The Dilemma

Lots of reading materials in academic content areas are difficult for even the best readers in the class! I wish there were an easy solution to this dilemma. However, I have found that students' comprehension of such texts can improve with sufficient comprehension strategy support before, during, and after their content reading.

First, segment the text into very small chunks, probably smaller chunks than seem necessary from your adult-reader point of view. Then get students to monitor their reading with the use of comprehension strategies.

To learn how to apply comprehension strategy instruction to your explicit content-area instruction, read on. This chapter provides many suggestions for explicit shared-reading instruction during social studies and science lessons. Use these scaffolds, too, during your literacy block for guided and independent reading.

Trade Books and Textbooks

Not so long ago, it was difficult to find nonfiction materials written on a primary level. But today, there are hundreds of nonfiction sources available for readers of all developmental stages, including young readers. I've used beautifully illustrated informational picture books to model the integration of comprehension strategies for students in kindergarten through eighth grade, using both the whole-class and small-group guided practice settings.

Many teachers have told me they would love to teach social studies exclusively through trade books (books published for the general public). But their school district mandates the use of particular textbooks. These teachers want to know how they can help their students apply comprehension strategies to their content area texts.

Reading textbooks can be more challenging than reading trade books. Historically, students have found textbooks to be less engaging. The textbook reading level, complete with lots of technical vocabulary, was often beyond the instructional level of many students. For young readers, the text structure in textbooks is generally less familiar than that of fiction. Furthermore, most content area reading is done with a whole class, rather than in small groups, with less teacher guidance to monitor the needs of struggling readers.

How can we fine-tune comprehension-strategy instruction to support students as they make meaning from required-reading sources, such as textbooks? The strategies outlined in this chapter, while they focus on the specific needs of students reading textbooks, are relevant to any informational text students may use, such as periodicals and trade books. The applications of integrated comprehension strategies in this instructional model will help your students become actively engaged before and during their nonfiction reading. That engagement becomes evident in their improved comprehension after reading.

This instructional model will help your students become actively engaged with the text, both before and during reading.

Broaden Your Perspective on Uses of Nonfiction (Informational Text) for Teaching Reading Comprehension

The materials students read in social studies or science classes are sometimes referred to as "nonfiction" and other times labeled, "expository." I use the term "informational text," which seems to cover the territory more broadly. It includes a range of text that is based in fact, including textbooks, trade books, biography, narrative nonfiction (information delivered through a story format), newspapers, magazines, as well as information available over the Internet.

We also need to broaden our definition of "text." We can all conjure up from our own academic past a visual image of a "textbook," a weighty tome of several hundred pages that droned on and on about some topic, about which we may have had only a vague interest. Outdated, black-and-white photos did little to pique our curiosity, and the lists of literal questions at the end of each chapter only added to the monotony of the reading, which was typically assigned as homework. Our text experience generally culminated with an end-of-chapter test that assessed how well we had committed the text's content to memory.

Today, informational text sports an updated look. The hefty "paperweights" with titles like *American History* and *Fourth Grade Science*, have trimmed down and are more focused. No longer do they cover a topic generally, or "objectively," but, instead, allow the author's voice to emerge as he or she embraces a few main points and draws the reader into the topic through the use of anecdotal elaboration to which young readers can relate on a more personal level. Add some glossy graphics: full-color photos, close-up cutaways, and interesting visual supports, and you've got texts with kid-appeal!

Whether you use a traditional social studies textbook or a more focused mini-text, you can use content-area reading assignments to help your students learn more about the reading process and more about themselves as readers, in addition to learning all those important content-related "facts" they need to know.

To bring the maximum benefit of these strategies to your students' comprehension of informational text, teach your students to apply comprehension strategies before, during, and after reading informational text, and be sure to use *all* the components of a comprehensive literacy program (shared, guided, and independent reading).

All of that reading doesn't have to occur during content area instruction. You might begin work on a particular strategy application with a whole-group, shared lesson from a chapter in the social studies text, such as, for an example, a textbook reading on the American Underground Railway of the 1800s. Then carry that topic forward in your literacy instruction in small-group guided reading using a related short text selection. The guided-reading text might be another expository selection (for example, an article from a *Kid's Discover* periodical), an easy-reader narrative nonfiction book (such as *The Daring Escape of Ellen Craft* by Cathy Moore), or a picture book biography (like *Minty: A Story of Young Harriet Tubman* by Alan Schroeder). Some students may be intrigued enough by what you're studying to want to carry that inquiry into further independent research.

See Chapter Seven for more information about using comprehension strategies during shared and guided-reading instruction. It will show you how to embed focused lessons on individual comprehension strategies applications into your comprehensive literacy program for the study of both fiction and informational text.

Getting Ready to Read Informational Text

Readers who simply "dive in" to informational text without a plan, without conscious consideration of what the task involves, are likely to have trouble comprehending the material. Even before students begin to read their informational texts, they should apply to their non-fiction reading assignments, such as chapters in their social studies or science textbook, the same comprehension strategies they've been using to understand fiction, such as novels, short stories and poems.

Some of the key distinctions between applying these strategies to fiction and to informational text lie in the kinds of predictions that students will need to make about the texts before they begin reading, as well as the types of connections that are most useful for students to make to the texts, the nature of the questions they should consider, the clues to meaning suggested by the text structure, and the way the graphics support students' understanding of the reading selection. The distinctions between applying reading strategies to informational text and to fiction are summarized in the chart on Page 89, "Getting My Mind Ready to Read: Worksheet for Applying Comprehension Strategies to Fiction and Nonfiction" (also available on the CD in the file titled, "SixA"). There are also mini-posters designed specifically for informational text strategy applications on pages 239–244 and on the CD file titled "SevenH."

Be sure to explain for your students in language they can easily understand the differences between getting ready to read fiction and getting ready to read informational text. One way to do this is to choose a text selection of each genre on the same basic topic. Then compare for your students the different ways they would prepare for each reading. I made this comparison meaningful to a class of fifth graders with two texts about dogs. The fictional narrative selection I used was the short story, "Stray," by Cynthia Rylant, from her anthology of short stories, *Every Living Thing* (Simon and Schuster, 1985). This class had already read the story as a shared reading experience. For the informational text piece, I chose a section from the book, *What is a Dog?*, from the series *The Science of Living Things* (Crabtree Publishing Company, 2000). On Page 90, the chart titled, "Getting My Mind Ready to Read: A Sample of How Some Fifth-Grade Students Completed the Worksheet for Applying Comprehension Strategies to Fiction and Nonfiction," shows how these students applied comprehension strategies to both texts. You could complete a similar chart with your students for paired texts (fiction and informational text) on any topic. A worksheet is provided on Page 91 for use by teachers and students applying the strategies specifically to nonfiction. (This worksheet is also available on the CD, in the file titled, "SixB".)

Using Comprehension Strategies with Informational Text during and after Reading

To use comprehension strategies productively during and after reading informational text, students should consider the special features of the text content and the structure of the text. On Page 92, the reference chart titled, "Using Comprehension Strategies: Focusing on Informational Text," shows how comprehension strategies can be used to activate student thinking about informational text. (This chart is also available in this chart on the CD, in the file titled, "SixC") The bulleted items in this chart can become the focus of individual comprehension strategy lessons. Again, the focus strategy should be integrated into the whole-strategy repertoire to empower readers even more fully.

We are now ready to put it all together! The next chapter will show you how to teach specific comprehension strategy applications using fiction and nonfiction through shared, guided, and independent reading.

Getting My Mind Ready to Read:
Applying Comprehension Strategies to Fiction and Nonfiction

Strategy	Getting My Mind Ready to Read Fiction	Getting My Mind Ready to Read Informational Text
Guessing/Predicting	What will probably happen in this story?	What will I probably learn from this text?
Connecting	What experiences have I had or what other books have I read that might relate to this story in some way?	What do I already know about this topic? (Schema)
Wondering	What will the problem be? How will the problem get solved?	What questions will this text probably answer? Are there subheadings that I can turn into questions?
Noticing	What other clues do I notice in this story that can help me: Do I know anything about the author or the topic? Are there lots of chapters/pages or just a few? Is there a blurb I can read on the back cover?	What clues do I notice in the way this text is written that might help me: Subheadings? Bolded or italicized words? Main idea statements? Side bars?
Picturing/Visualizing	Are there any illustrations? Can they help me predict the story?	Are there any graphics, such as maps, charts, pictures, graphs? What details do I notice in each graphic? How do I think these graphics might relate to the text?
Figuring Out	Does it look like this story will be easy or difficult to read? Can I read it quickly, or should I read it slowly?	Does it look like this text will be easy or difficult to read? Can I read it quickly, or should I read it slowly?

Getting My Mind Ready to Read:
A Sample of How Some Fifth Grade Students Completed the Worksheet for Applying Comprehension Strategies to Fiction and Nonfiction

Strategy	Getting My Mind Ready to Read Fiction: *Stray*	Getting My Mind Ready to Read Informational Text: *Dogs' Super Senses*
Guessing/Predicting	What will this story probably be about? *This story will probably be about a dog that doesn't have a home.*	What will I probably learn from this text? *I think I will learn about dogs' senses in this chapter. Other chapters will tell me other kinds of information about dogs.*
Connecting	What experiences have I had or what other books have I read that might relate to this story in some way? *Once there was a dog in my yard that just kept hanging around. We didn't think it had a home, but my dad wouldn't let us keep it because we already have 2 dogs.*	What do I already know about this topic? *I'm pretty sure I remember learning that dogs have a really great sense of hearing; they can hear things even when they're far away. I'm not sure about their other senses.*
Wondering	What will the problem be? How will the problem get solved? *I wonder if this dog is going to find a home. I wonder if a child will ask to keep it.*	What questions will this text probably answer? Are there subheadings I can turn into questions? *I think this chapter will answer questions like: Do dogs have good eyesight? Do dogs have a strong sense of smell?*
Noticing	What other clues do I notice in this story that can help me: Do I know anything about the author? Are there lots of chapters/pages or just a few? *This story is only about 5 pages long, so I can probably read it in one sitting. It is written by Cynthia Rylant and I know she usually creates interesting characters in her writing.*	What clues do I notice in the way this text is written that might help me: Subheadings? Bolded or italicized words? Main idea statements? Side bars? *This text is broken up into paragraphs like "All the Better to Smell You." That one must be about a dog's sense of smell. The subheadings give good clues.*
Picturing/Visualizing	Are there any illustrations? Can they help me predict the story? *There is only one tiny picture on the first page. The dog looks sad, but I can't tell much more from such a small picture.*	Are there any graphics? What kinds: Maps, charts, photos, graphs? What details do I notice in each graphic? How do I think these graphics might relate to the text? *There are three photos of dogs. One shows a dog with huge eyes; another shows a dog with his nose in the ground; another shows a dog with his ears perked up, like he's listening. So maybe this chapter is going to talk about a dog's sense of hearing, sight, and smell.*
Figuring Out	Does it look like this story will be easy or difficult to read? Can I read it quickly or should I read it slowly? *I think this will be an easy story for me, but I should read it slowly enough to get all the information I can about the characters.*	Does it look like this text will be easy or difficult to read? Can I read it quickly or should I read it slowly? *There are lots of clues to help me understand this chapter. But I need to read each paragraph carefully enough to figure out its main idea and details.*

| | | Name _____ | Date: _____ |

Getting My Mind Ready to Read:
Worksheet for Applying Comprehension Strategies to Nonfiction

Strategy	Getting My Mind Ready To Read Informational Text	Getting My Mind Ready to read _____ Title
Guessing/Predicting	What will I probably learn from this text?	
Connecting	What do I already know about this topic?	
Wondering	What questions will this text probably answer? Are there subheadings I can turn into questions?	
Noticing	What clues do I notice in the way this text is written that might help me? Subheadings? Bolded or italicized words? Main idea statements? Side bars?	
Picturing/Visualizing	Are there any graphics? Maps, charts, pictures, graphs? What details do I notice in each graphic? How do I think these graphics might relate to the text?	
Figuring Out	Does it look like this text will be easy or difficult to read? Can I read it quickly or should I read it slowly?	

Using Comprehension Strategies: Focusing on Informational Text

Strategy	Possible Focus Lessons
Guessing/Predicting	• Where might I find answers to my questions that are not answered in this reading? • What might be the outcome of [this event?] • What information from this reading do I predict I will remember the longest? Why?
Connecting	**People** • Are the people in this reading at all like me or like anyone I know? Explain. • How do I feel about these people? (Like them, dislike them, admire them) Why? **Times and places** • Have I ever been somewhere like this place? How is it similar to or different from where I live? • Would I like to see or live in this place? • What would I like or not like about living during this time? **Events** • Did the people in this situation handle the problem the way I would have handled it? • What might I have done differently to solve this situation
Wondering	• What questions can I ask about this reading, questions that begin with who, what, when, where, why, how? • What questions are answered in this reading? • What questions are not answered in this reading?
Noticing	• Am I noticing all of the important clues to meaning (lists, definitions, people's names, special events, dates, places)? • Am I noticing the important clue words that help me answer my questions? • Am I noticing when I don't "get it?"
Picturing/Visualizing	• Can I make a picture in my mind of the new vocabulary words? • What pictures do I have in my mind of the people, places, and events that I am reading about? • Could I explain to someone else how the graphics are important to this reading?
Figuring Out	• If I wanted to really impress somebody about how much I know about this topic now, what would I say? What are some of the "big" words I would use? • What questions might be on a test about this reading? • What would be some good questions from this reading for the game show Jeopardy? • How would I rate my understanding of this reading? (high, middle, low) • How did I help myself when I got stuck in this reading? • How do all the clues fit together to help me understand this reading? • Why is this information important? • If I could only remember a few things from this reading, what would I want to remember? • If I had to explain this information to a younger kid, how would I explain it so the child would understand?

7

Teaching Reading Comprehension Strategies in Shared, Guided, and Independent Reading

Teach focused comprehension strategy lessons during all parts of your literacy block: shared, guided, and independent reading.

Teach focused lessons in specific comprehension strategy applications.

Plan ahead to get the greatest benefit from strategy instruction during shared and guided reading. Templates for planning and sample planners for both shared and guided reading lessons are included in this chapter in both paper format and electronic format.

Provide explicit instruction *before* assigning tasks for students to undertake independently or in small groups.

Developing a Well Balanced Reading Program

In too many classrooms, comprehension strategy instruction does not play any role in shared, guided, or independent reading, much less in all three components of a literacy program. In many classrooms, use of one element of a literacy program predominates in what should be a balanced, three-way approach to literacy instruction. And teachers view instruction in reading comprehension as "something extra" that must be added to an already crammed literacy curriculum.

But what could be more central to reading than comprehension? Comprehension strategy instruction can and should, therefore, play a central role in all parts of your literacy program.

Too often, teachers tell me, "We don't have explicit comprehension strategy instruction in our school; we have guided reading." They imagine that comprehension strategy instruction is incompatible with guided reading. Their classroom reading programs are likely to focus primarily on guided reading in small groups. And they wonder how and where time can be made available for other kinds of literacy experiences.

At other schools, I've heard, "We do reader's workshop in our district." That statement sometimes reveals a single-minded focus on independent reading and conferring, with little shared or small-group guided work.

And at other times, teachers tell me their district uses a literature-based basal system or relies on "core" books. That kind of system of instruction usually means that every child in the class will read the same text at the same time. In such cases, it is almost certain that the reading will be so far beyond the reach of some students that the text must be read to them, skewing the instruction heavily toward a shared-reading approach.

It is unwise and shortsighted to develop reading programs that revolve around a single focus, whether guided reading, reader's workshop, basal reading texts, or core books. The focus should be providing good literacy instruction and finding a way to balance shared, guided, and independent reading. You need all three aspects of reading to have a vital reading program.

Described below is the role of each of these "three faces of reading" in comprehension instruction and the limitations of each, too.

The Three Faces of Reading Instruction
If I were to wander into your classroom any morning during the school year, it is likely that I would see children "doing reading" in one of three ways: shared reading, guided reading, or independent reading. The charts below describe what each reading scenario might look like, as well as its strengths and relative limitations. Review these three charts to get a sense of the contrasting and complementary ways in which these three approaches to "doing reading" help your students to become better readers.

Shared Reading

In the classroom you'll see	How it helps students	Limitations
Teacher working with the whole class (often)	Provides access to interesting or important text that may be beyond students' reading level	Difficult for teacher to monitor and assess students' growth as readers since the whole class is taught as one large group
Teacher reading aloud (often)	Provides students incidental opportunities for learning vocabulary and text content	Student focus is on listening, rather than reading, so students' reading needs are addressed only indirectly
Students interacting with the text in some way (possibly participating in the reading)	Provides some opportunities for students to think critically about text	Teacher remains in charge of the learning; hence, there is limited release of responsibility (Students don't move toward independent use of reading strategies)
Teachers and students thinking aloud	Provides opportunities for teachers to model comprehension strategies and provides some opportunities for students to think aloud	This format will not likely provide sufficient opportunity for reticent or struggling readers to actively participate
Use of short texts or excerpts of texts — such as chapters (including picture books and big books)	Provides opportunities for students to focus on texts or portions of text that are particularly challenging	Some text selections may be beyond the cognitive capacity of some students in the class
Some use of texts beyond students' instructional reading level	Provides access to content that may be beyond students' reading level, but within their range of interest	Teacher may need to provide extra scaffolding to students in decoding or comprehending the text if it is beyond either their independent or instructional level

I encourage you to consult my Annotated Bibliographies of Children's Literature, especially the bibliography titled, "Texts for Use in Blended Strategy Practice and Guided Strategy Applications," on page 218, where you will find many entries for books especially well suited to teacher modeling of comprehension strategies during shared reading.

Guided Reading

In the classroom you'll see	How it helps students	Limitations
Small-group instruction	Provides for engagement, participation, and collaboration of all group members	Focus is mostly on practice, not independent application
Use of reading materials at students' instructional level	The degree of challenge in instructional-level materials demonstrates to students that comprehension strategies are useful in unlocking meaning in text	Requires that teacher has good classroom management techniques to assure all students' active engagement in literacy learning, including students not in ongoing small-group session
Lots of use of short texts, various genres	Provides for explicit instruction, leading students toward independence through extensive student practice with application of strategies	Students read a limited amount of text
Dialogue among group members, including teacher, in the process of negotiating a shared meaning of text	Provides for close teacher monitoring of students' progress and provides opportunities for all students in group to think critically	Requires careful planning by teacher to make teacher-guided small-group sessions a regular, consistent part of literacy instruction for all students in classroom

Again, I encourage you to consult my Annotated Bibliographies of Children's Literature, especially the bibliography titled, "Texts for Use in Blended Strategy Practice and Guided Strategy Applications," on page 218.

Independent Reading

In the classroom you'll see	How it helps students	Limitations
Students reading alone or in pairs	Provides for student choice in text selection and engagement with texts that are at their independent reading level	If text selections are not monitored by teacher, students may select books that are too difficult for them to read independently
Students meeting with a small group without the teacher present (literature circles or book clubs)	Provides opportunity for student collaboration (literature circles, book clubs)	May lead to superficial discussion (whether verbal or written) about text if students do not have a good grasp of comprehension strategies
Teacher conferring with individual students or "listening in" on small-group book talks	Provides opportunity for students' independent application of reading strategies	Difficult for teachers to get around to confer with all students
Frequent use of "chapter books" (though texts of all lengths may be used)	Provides opportunities for students to engage with longer texts and can help with their reading fluency	If students do not self-monitor while they read a longer text, they can easily lose track of meaning.

This book does not contain any bibliography of texts for independent reading assignments. The possibilities for such assignments are so vast that it would be nearly impossible to compile a list that in any way represents even a small sampling of the best books appropriate for any grade level.

As you select chapter books for your students to read independently, keep in mind characteristics of texts that appeal to children at the age you are teaching. Look for texts that will expose your young readers to a variety of genres and a variety of authors. And always, always consider the reading level. Remember that books that students read independently should be easier than books you use to teach reading. Students should be able to decode and understand their independent reading books with ease, on their own.

Including Comprehension Strategy Instruction Throughout the Reading Block

As you can see from the three charts above, when teachers emphasize one way of "doing reading" at the expense of the other two, the result is an anemic literacy curriculum, a curriculum that lacks full-blooded vitality. To offer students a robust literacy curriculum, teachers must fully implement all three approaches. Incorporating explicit strategy applications into your shared, guided, and independent reading will keep the instructional focus squarely on *comprehension* — right where it should be.

To support your students and help them fine-tune their reading strategy use, read on. The following section shows what target strategy application looks like in classrooms where shared, guided, and independent reading are all emphasized.

A Look at the Instructional Model

We can begin our morning with shared reading and move to guided instruction and independent application — all with comprehension strategy instruction as our main focus. Our literacy block could look something like the three-phase model on the next page (a model described in detail on pages 100–109).

An Instructional Model
For Shared, Guided, and Independent Reading

Phase I (20 – 30 minutes)

Shared reading occurs daily or several times per week with the entire class and targets an application of a specific strategy.

Phase II (Two components operate concurrently) (60 – 75 minutes)

Guided-reading sessions offer students the opportunity for intensive, guided practice with the "target" strategy used in the shared-reading lesson. These small-group sessions also provide opportunities for students to apply *all* comprehension strategies, as well as other skills and strategies of proficient reading. The group, which includes the teacher, will use a short text or an excerpt of a longer text. The teacher will meet with two or three small groups each day in sessions lasting 20-30 minutes. Groups of struggling readers should meet with the teacher as many days during the week as possible while more competent readers may do fine with two-to-three sessions each week. By the end of the week, *all* students in the class should have met at least twice with their guided-reading group.

Independent reading is a daily component of this instructional model, with three or four longer texts selected collaboratively by teacher and students. Independent reading may allow individual students to read on their own or in a small group, where peer collaboration can reinforce the strategy applications modeled in the shared-reading lesson. During the independent reading time, students may also engage in other literacy-related work, including written reflection on strategy use and written response to literature. If the literacy block is long enough (more than two hours), a writer's workshop, focusing on the process and craft of writing, may also be incorporated into Phase II.

Phase III (10 – 15 minutes)

Reflection. All students in the class come back together to share insights related to the day's target-strategy application from shared, guided, and independent reading.

How the Model Works in a Classroom

Phase I: Shared Reading

Too many teachers imagine that effective explicit instruction needs to come in brief "sound bytes" of ten minutes or less. (In one district an administrator actually confessed to me that until recently, teachers in her district received a written reprimand if their lessons exceeded the ten–minute limit.) But thorough teaching, the kind that begins with a clear explanation, provides careful modeling, and begins to release responsibility to the learner through structured practice, may require lessons of more than a ten–minute duration. Some shared-reading sessions won't take as much as 20-25 minutes. And that will leave more time for other phases of the reading block. However, when your shared-reading lesson is purring along and everyone is absorbed in it, don't stop because you imagine these precious minutes are not being spent productively.

Here's one example from a classroom I visited recently, where one of my favorite third-grade teachers, Nicole Brown, flagged me down as I was walking past her classroom doorway. She held a picture book in her hand. "How about giving me a hand with something?" she asked.

As I joined her in her classroom, I found 25 third graders sitting cross-legged on a rug in the reading corner. Nicole explained to me, "We're beginning our theme about *Characters and People with a Special Passion*, and I wanted to use this book. Any ideas about how I might get started?"

The book was *Snowflake Bentley* by Jacqueline Briggs Martin. I love *Snowflake Bentley* although I certainly hadn't anticipated teaching a lesson with it on this particular morning. But I agreed. "Okay," I said. "I'll teach this first lesson. And tomorrow I'll come back and coach you through a similar lesson of your own."

Then I settled into the old wooden rocking chair in the reading corner. My mind raced to find a place to begin. For our shared reading today, I decided to think aloud for the students about our focus-strategy application, *noticing characterization*.

"I have a *passion* for chocolate, summer days at the beach, and cozy slippers," I told the attentive third graders who sat before me. "What do you suppose *passion* means?" I asked them.

The students figured out right away that a *passion* was something someone cares about a lot. So I continued. "This morning we're going to use our *noticing* strategy. We're going to notice what a character does or says or thinks so we can find *clues* to what is important to him or her."

After naming the strategy, *noticing*, and its particular application, *characterization*, we discussed a bit more about *what* this strategy was and *how* and *when* good readers use this strategy during reading. Students must understand the process of a particular strategy application if they are to improve in their use of the strategy. In this example, I defined the strategy for noticing characterization by explaining to my young charges that authors almost never come right out and tell readers what is important to a character. Instead, authors show what is important to a character by including details about the character's life, such as thoughts, actions, feelings and circumstances. It's the reader's job to read carefully enough to find (notice) all of these clues to meaning. Finding (noticing) the best clues is a little like a treasure hunt. And this strategy is very important because, without evidence from the text, your guesses may not be accurate. When you guess that a character *cares about* something, you must present the details, the clues you have gathered from the text, to support your point of view.

"This is how *I* look for clues about a character as I read," I told them. Then I found a dry-erase marker and wrote the following list on a portable white board:

1. I read slowly and carefully; I don't rush.
2. When I come to an interesting detail, I pause and ask myself, *Why did the author include this information? What is the author trying to show me?*
3. As I continue my reading, I keep in mind the clues that I have already found.
4. When I get to the end of the reading, I think about how all the clues fit together. Do they "add up" to some big idea? What is this "big idea?"
5. Once I've *figured out* the main idea, I go back and reread to see if I've overlooked any really great clues during my first reading.

I followed my explanation with modeling the application of this strategy, *noticing*, to characterization. At places in the text where I noticed interesting details about Wilson Bentley's life, I paused to think aloud for

Students must understand the process of a particular strategy application if they are to improve in their use of the strategy.

the class about the evidence I found of Bentley's passion, snowflakes. I expected students would begin to *notice* some of this evidence themselves as I proceeded through the text. They listened to me model for a few pages. Then, as I expected, they began to raise their hands to add their voices to the ideas I had located. They told me,

"He said snowflakes were as beautiful as butterflies."

"He used his microscope to look at snow and thought the patterns were more beautiful than he imagined."

"When he got his camera to work, he said, 'Now everyone can see the great beauty in a crystal.'"

"His snow crystal pictures were his favorites."

"He wrote about snow and gave speeches about it."

Their classroom teacher, Nicole, is an experienced teacher of comprehension strategies. And it immediately became obvious to me as I listened to her students' answers that they were quite familiar with all of the basic reading strategies from their practice blending strategies together. And they were also familiar with the think-aloud process.

Still, intermediate-grade readers almost universally need to learn to identify evidence in text to support their conclusions. So I knew our time discussing this application of the *noticing* strategy would be time well spent. And we concluded the session with some reflection on our lesson so that everyone could appreciate *why* applying the *noticing* strategy to characterization is so important to good comprehension. I began by asking the students why *they* thought *noticing* details about a character is important. They soon began to explain to me that when they took time to think about a character's specific thoughts, words, and actions, they could more easily reach a conclusion about what the character values most. And, as I pointed out for them, understanding the characters in the story makes it much easier to understand the story.

Snowflake Bentley was a perfect picture book to use for this shared-reading lesson on *noticing details that reveal character traits.* There were in this fascinating text many examples of the kinds of evidence needed to "prove it in the text." And now that the children had watched me model this strategy application and had tried their hand at applying it themselves through the less demanding role of *listener*, they would attempt the strategy as *readers* during guided reading with a teacher and then during independent reading on their own.

Phase II: Guided and Independent Reading (60-75 minutes)
Following the shared-reading lesson, some students would work
independently on literacy tasks at their seats while I met consecutively
with two different guided reading groups. But before the class broke up
for these different activities, I made sure they understood the nature of
the literacy task ahead of all of them, to *notice details of
characterization*, specifically, to identify in their text details that
demonstrate the special passion of one character.

I gave a specific assignment to the students engaged in independent
reading. "Each of you should find three places in your 'just right book'
that show something about the special *passion* of one of the characters.
Then mark each of these details with a sticky-note and decide what these
details *show*. I'll ask you to share what you've found during our
reflecting time later."

"This assignment will work really well with the four books they're
reading," Nicole commented to me. In her class, independent reading
doesn't mean entirely individual book selection. She makes four book
choices available, and her students pick the one they think is "just right"
for them (and sometimes their selections are aided by a little guidance
from Nicole.)

- **Student's Role in Selecting Text for Independent Reading**
  With the plan Nicole uses in her classroom, an arrangement I
  recommend, students choose from a small selection of books that the
  teacher has made available for their independent reading work. And
  the student choices are mediated by the teacher, who knows both the
  reading level and reading interests of her students and is also familiar
  with the texts.

  What young readers lose in autonomy in such an arrangement they
  gain in richness of literacy experience due to the teacher's skilled
  guidance. Additionally, the teacher can more easily manage to read all
  four of the texts, increasing the likelihood of meaningful teacher
  monitoring of student reading progress. Also, as with the guided-
  reading component, when several classmates are reading the same
  book, opportunities abound for student collaboration, including the
  use of literature circles and book clubs.

  Of course, aside from the specific instructional goals of this
  comprehension strategy learning model, students should always be
  encouraged to read books of their own choice. And some of their

reading for pleasure can and should occur within the school day. But it doesn't have to happen during the execution of this instructional model. Not everything a child reads can or should be absorbed into the academic curriculum.

- **Conferring with Students**

  The reader's workshop model of literacy instruction promotes the notion that teachers need to meet with students one-on-one to assess their progress as readers. While this goal is worthy, it may not always be realistic. And you will likely find that the small-group, guided reading sessions adequately meet both the students' and the teacher's needs for such conferences.

  If you have 25 students and spend a full 100 minutes per day on independent reading, that's 500 minutes per week. Divide that by your 25 kids and you have a whopping 20 minutes (maximum) to devote to any one reader. If you met with each of them individually, you would spend your entire literacy block conferring! If you steal a few moments here and there for some shared reading or reflection, you could end up with a mere ten minutes of quality conferencing with one child in an entire week. Or you could spend 20 minutes with that child every two weeks. And that is just not enough.

  And under such an arrangement, the actual quality of the student-teacher interaction would be questionable since not even the most voracious reader-teacher can keep up with the literary diets of a whole class of readers. You would not likely show up at a book club meeting with a group of your friends without having read the book. If you did, you wouldn't be able to contribute much to the conversation; your insights would be superficial at best. But teachers show up for one-on-one student book conferences all the time with only a sketchy knowledge of the content their student has read. If you ask, "Tell me what you've learned about the main character," it's difficult to assess the student's answer when you don't know anything about that character. And asking questions like, "Where are you having trouble?" doesn't do much for the child who doesn't realize she's having a problem.

  Instead of trying to hurdle such practical limitations of meeting with your students in one-on-one book conferences, I encourage you to rely with confidence on the much more comfortable and very effective format of small-group, guided reading sessions to assess your students' reading strengths and needs.

During small-group instruction, you will have the opportunity to observe closely as your students work together to construct meaning. You may note that Joshua is wonderful with connections, but fails to create useful visual images. You may see that the entire group is having a problem noticing important ideas in informational text. And you can determine who is using their comprehension strategies to learn from their reading, construct meaning, and interpret text, and who can articulate the strategies, but still can't think critically about what they have read.

When a teacher is meeting 75 – 90 minutes per week with each group (over the course of two-to-five meeting sessions each week) he or she can make these kinds of discoveries about student progress and watch students interact with the text as well as with the other students in the small group. Student conversation with peers in these reading-and-discussion groups will inevitably bring multiple points of view into focus for each student, allowing a true critical perspective to begin to emerge.

Student conversations with peers in small groups will bring multiple points of view into focus.

A Small Group Guided Reading Primer

Small-group guided reading sessions are the teacher's best opportunity to reinforce *all* of the skills and strategies essential to proficient reading — not just the metacognitive strategies. These groups provide an ideal format for focusing on vocabulary and word work, such as decoding skills, structural analysis of words, or even parts of speech. Within the small group, a teacher can also observe and address students' reading fluency and the kinds of comprehension questions that readers ought to consider *after* they have achieved an initial understanding of a text, questions related to theme, characters' motives and the author's point of view.

But all of this work will not happen within a single guided reading session. Depending on the length and complexity of the text the small group is using, a thorough guided reading instructional sequence might extend over two to five sessions in the course of one week.

During the two guided reading sessions I conducted on my morning in Nicole's classroom, I limited the length of each session to no longer than 25 minutes. In each group, we focused on the application of the *noticing* strategy, specifically, noticing evidence of the overriding passion of the main character.

In terms of choosing a text to use in the small groups, I located a couple of poems written at these students' instructional level and full of textual evidence of the passion of the main character. And we also thought aloud about *all* of our strategies using the cue-cards available on our reading table. But I paid especially close attention to the kind of *noticing* that had been the target of our shared reading that morning, *noticing* evidence in the text of the main character's passion.

The poems I chose for that morning's small groups were short and simple enough to accomplish both the *before* and *during* guided reading components in one session. The poem I used with Nicole's group of strongest readers was "Myrtle," by Ted Kooser in *One World at a Time* (1985):

> *Wearing her yellow rubber slicker,*
> *Myrtle, our* Journal *carrier,*
> *has come early through rain and darkness*
> *to bring us the news.*
> *A woman of thirty or so,*
> *with three small children at home,*
> *she's told me she likes*
> *a long walk by herself in the morning.*
> *And with pride in her work,*
> *she's wrapped the news neatly in plastic —*
> *a bread bag, beaded with rain,*
> *that reads WONDER.*
> *From my doorway I watch her*
> *flicker from porch to porch as she goes,*
> *a yellow candle flame*
> *no wind or weather dare extinguish.*

As eight students found their places at our table, I scanned the text and found about four words that might be unfamiliar to students (slicker, pride, flicker, extinguish), as well as a few other words important to the meaning of the poem in some way (Journal, porch, plastic, beaded). I jotted them on the white board.

"Who has an idea how these words might connect to this poem" I asked. And a lot of students volunteered their thoughts, which gave me a pretty good idea about the extent of their prior knowledge concerning these concepts. It also helped them make predictions and set a purpose for their reading:

"Maybe Myrtle is a kid who kept a journal."

"Maybe the journal was beaded."

"Maybe Myrtle had to extinguish a fire."

We agreed that the title gave us little information upon which to base our predictions. And since these students weren't familiar with this author, we couldn't glean any clues from that source. While I wanted to prepare everyone in our group for the reading ahead, I didn't want to supply so much up-front information that the actual reading became redundant. So we moved right into the text.

Robert, age nine, placed each of the cue-cards face-up on the table. Since this poem was short and the students had an above average reading level, I decided we would attack it in one piece. The kids read the text silently and then lunged for their cue-card-of-choice. I was prepared to jump in with a few prompts to remind them to *notice details that lead to an understanding of character traits.* But no such nudging was needed.

These students willingly shared their connections and mental pictures. And I was especially curious to hear from the two students who held the *noticing* cards. Alisha, in that very articulate manner so typical of bright little girls, stated, "I noticed that Myrtle wrapped the paper in a plastic bag." Then Manny, a diminutive third grader wearing a sweatshirt that looked to be twice his size, glanced up at me for the first time. Until this point, he'd seemed more focused on the deep study of his pencil than the study of the text. But now he wanted to talk. "I noticed that Myrtle had three small children at home," he said.

We had a solid start!

So I asked the students, "Did anyone notice any other detail of Myrtle's life?" As the children's hands shot up, I erased our vocabulary words from the white board and recorded the ideas that they offered:
"Myrtle likes to take long walks."
"She wears a yellow slicker."

When Reggie said he wasn't sure what a *slicker* is, Alisha announced, "It's a raincoat!"

Soon our white board was covered with the details of characterization that these children had *noticed* in the poem.

Then I asked them, "What kind of a person was Myrtle? What were her passions?"

Manny, looking pensive with a furrowed brow, studied the ideas I had scrawled on the board: "Well, she was passionate about her job as a newspaper carrier," he said. "Look at the evidence; she took the time to wrap the newspapers in plastic bags so they wouldn't get wet, and she made sure all her customers got their paper, even in bad weather. She didn't mind that she had to do all that walking every morning."

For me, this was one of those magical moments in teaching. I could see in Manny's careful observations plenty of evidence that he was learning how to use reading strategies to understand text. Finding and then using evidence in text to derive an inference is an important goal that we'd like all our students to achieve. Too often, however, teachers conclude that young children are incapable of finding such concrete details in text and then transforming them into an abstract idea, like personal passion. But when our teaching is careful and focused and we set the bar high enough, we are very often rewarded with brilliance from even our youngest learners.

I met with one other small group during this morning in Nicole's classroom. These students were not as advanced as the first group had been, but with a poem at their instructional level, they were able to achieve a similar degree of success with this same strategy.

Phase III: Concluding the Lesson with Reflection
Once you've completed Phase II of this instructional model, the independent and small-group literacy activities, give your students the opportunity to reflect on what they've learned. Good reading-strategy lessons are not over until students have discussed their learning process.

In my visit to Nicole Brown's third-grade classroom, I concluded our reading lesson by rounding up the whole class. The students came back to the rug-area of the room from their desks or from the several beanbag chairs located in various corners of the room, where they had been busy with independent reading assignments.

"Nice work, everyone," I said. "Did anyone find any great evidence today in your independent reading book?"

Almost every hand shot up. And the class listened attentively as several children (not just the best readers) turned to the pages that bore their sticky-notes and then read their evidence aloud. It was plain to me as I watched and listened that, as a result of our shared, independent and guided reading that morning, every child in the class had gotten a little better at *noticing* significant details in text in order to *figure out* information about a character, information that the author hadn't explicitly stated.

I wrapped up the session by eliciting student answers to four questions.
• What was hard about applying this strategy?
• What was easy?
• If you had to explain this strategy, *noticing*, to a third grader in another classroom, what would you say?
• Why do you think this strategy is important to understanding what you read?

Good strategy lessons are not over until students have discussed their learning process.

These kinds of questions, posed at the conclusion of the literacy block, allow students to discuss the learning process and to reflect about more than just what they *liked* about a book (the typical discussion topic in many intermediate-grade classrooms). This process of questioning and reflection, specifically in regards to the focused application of a reading strategy, helps students remember what they've learned so they can apply it independently as they read subsequent texts.

To further support student thinking on what they've read, I offer on the next page some additional questions teachers can use after shared, guided, or independent reading. "Questions for Reflecting on the Reading Process," also available on the CD in files titled "SevenA," will help students to reflect on both the reading process and the content of a text.

Questions for Reflecting on the Reading Process

(For group sharing and individual conferences)

Reflecting on the reading process (questions that are important to ask every day):

- What did you do today during independent reading and writing?
- How have these activities helped you become a better reader and writer?
- What will be your next learning step? (What should you work on tomorrow?)

Other questions to ask about the reading process:

- Why was this text a good choice for focusing on this strategy? If you feel it was not a good text for focusing on this strategy, please explain why.
- Was this a text that needed to be read slowly? Or could it be read quickly? Why?
- Do you consider this text easy or difficult? Why?
- Which parts of this text were the most interesting? Why?
- How did the author make this text interesting?
- Was this text similar to any other text you have read? How?
- What kind of person would probably enjoy this text? Why?
- Do you think the author had to do any research in order to write this? Explain.
- How would you like to share your strategic thinking about this text? (with a partner, with a group of students in a literature circle, with the whole class, in writing)
- Find an example of a scene in this text that you can visualize. What made this scene easy to picture?
- What strategies helped you the most to understand this text? Explain.

Questions to ask about the ideas in a text:

- What three questions would you use to evaluate a student's understanding of this text.
- A question I still have after reading this is _____.
- Would this be a good text for a child older than you to read? Explain.
- Could it be read by a younger child? Explain.
- What ideas in this reading really stand out to you? Why do these ideas stand out?
- Would you like to read something else on this same topic? By the same author? Explain.
- Think of another good title for this text selection. Why would this be a good title?
- What did you learn from this reading that you will want to remember for a long time?
- How did this text make you feel? Explain.
- Compare this text to another text that is similar in some way. Which did you like better? Why?
- What would you like to ask this author or illustrator? Why?
- What did the author of this text care about? How can you tell?
- What text would you pair with this one for students to read together? Why do you think these texts would go well together?

**Teacher Planning
for Shared, Guided, and Independent Reading**

As I move through all three phases of the literacy block, I try to convey an easygoing spontaneity and a sense that we, teacher and students, are learners together, unraveling the magic and mysteries of great literature. The truth is, however, that your students' success with reading strategies depends a lot on *you*, their teacher, being familiar with the texts you assign, as well as your careful preparation of plans for shared and guided reading so that the lessons are delivered both efficiently and effectively.

Although creating written plans for teaching reading comprehension strategies may seem like one more chore, teachers often tell me that their instruction is richer due to the time they've spent putting their plans on paper. They say the plan keeps them focused. And the act of considering all the options beforehand makes their instruction intentional, rather than incidental. Furthermore, once your plans have been developed, it's easy to pull them out to use again in subsequent school years.

You may want to use the "Shared Reading Planner: Explaining and Modeling a Strategy Thoroughly" (page 113 and on the CD in the file titled, "SevenB"). It illustrates how to plan for the lesson just described about *Snowflake Bentley*. Or develop your own shared reading lesson using the "Shared Reading Planner" template on page 114 (also available on the CD in the file titled, "SevenC").

On pages 115–118, you will find an example of a "Multi-Day Guided Reading Planner" based on the group that read "Myrtle." The planner includes a cover sheet and three separate templates, one each for *before, during,* and *after* reading. The blank "Multi-Day Guided Reading Planner" templates follow on pages 119–122. (These planning templates are also available on the CD in the file titled, "SevenD.") Use these to plan your own intermediate grade level guided instruction.

Also regarding planning, I encourage you to make time for professional development with your colleagues, writing teaching plans that you can share with each other. One day of work by twenty teachers, working at or around the same grade level, can yield twenty shared and guided reading planners. That's about twenty weeks' worth of curriculum!

What if some aspects of this model don't work for me in my classroom? The model I've suggested here is only *one way* of putting principles of quality shared, guided, and independent literacy instruction into practice. There are as many ways of teaching well as there are teachers. After I rattle on about how I would conduct shared or guided or independent reading, teachers are sometimes hesitant to say, "This guided reading phase doesn't quite work in my classroom the way you've organized it." Or, "I've changed independent reading to also include . . . . ."

That's okay. In fact, it's better than okay because your adjustments can allow this model to work most effectively in your classroom, with your students, considering *your* teaching style. As I often tell teachers, "Right after I get over my feelings of rejection because you aren't doing things *my* way, I'm glad that you haven't taken my ideas mindlessly into your classroom like some kind of recipe for reading comprehension instruction. When you adapt this model to *your* particular needs, I know that you have thought critically enough about the content to feel comfortable taking a stand on what *you* believe to be right for the children *you* teach."

With that caveat in mind, the following lesson planners may prove helpful in bringing explicit instruction in reading comprehension strategies into your classroom and your literacy program.

SHARED READING PLANNER
Explaining and Modeling a Strategy Thoroughly

Title of text used for lesson: *Snowflake Bentley* by Jacqueline Briggs Martin

Before reading, provide an explanation of the strategy that includes the following:

- Name the strategy application:
  Notice what a character does or says or thinks to provide clues to the things that are important to him or her.

- Explain the strategy (***What*** is it?)
  Authors almost never come right out and <u>tell</u> readers what is important to a character. Authors <u>show</u> what is important by including details about the character's life. It's the reader's job to read carefully enough to find all of these clues to meaning. Finding the best clues is a little like a treasure hunt.

- Explain ***how*** you use the strategy (Offer simple steps)
  1. Read slowly and carefully; don't rush.
  2. When you come to an interesting detail, pause and ask yourself, *Why did the author include this information? What is the author trying to show me?*
  3. Remember the clues that you have found as you continue to read.
  4. When you get to the end of the reading, see how all the clues fit together. Do they "add up" to some big idea? What is this "big idea?"
  5. Once you've figured out the main idea, go back and reread and see if you overlooked any really great clues during your first reading.

- Explain ***when*** good readers use this strategy (Before, during, after reading)
  This is a strategy that good readers use <u>during</u> reading when they need to <u>find evidence</u> for something. Maybe they have to find evidence about a character—-or something else in a text.

Note some places within the text where you intend to pause to model the use of this strategy <u>during</u> reading:
He said snowflakes were as beautiful as butterflies.
He used his microscope to look at snow and thought the patterns were more beautiful than he imagined.
When he got his camera to work, he said, "Now everyone can see the great beauty in a crystal."
His snow crystal pictures were his favorites.
He wrote about snow and gave speeches about it.

<u>After</u> reading: Reflect on *why* this strategy is important to good comprehension
This strategy is important because answers without evidence are not very good answers at all.
When you say that a character *cares about* something, you need reasons to support your opinion.

SHARED READING PLANNER:
Explaining and Modeling a Strategy Thoroughly

Title of text used for lesson: _____

<u>Before</u> reading, provide an explanation of the strategy that includes the following:
- Name the strategy application:

- Define the strategy (***What*** is it?):

- Explain ***how*** good readers use the strategy (Offer simple steps):

- Explain ***when*** good readers use this strategy (Before, during, after reading):

Note some places within the text where you intend to pause to model the use of this strategy <u>during</u> reading:

<u>After</u> reading: Reflect on *why* this strategy is important to good comprehension

MULTI-DAY GUIDED READING PLAN:
Supporting Students *Before*, *During*, and *After* Reading at their <u>Instructional</u> Level

Text: <u>*Myrtle*   by Ted Kooser</u>   **Genre:** <u>   Poetry   </u>

This text is part of a: ___Genre study   ___Author study   _X_ Theme study

Title of study: <u>Characters and People with Special Passions</u>

This packet contains:

Pre-reading Plan for Guided Reading
- Prior knowledge questions to ask to get students ready to read

- Predictions to encourage

- Purpose to establish

- Vocabulary to teach

During Reading Plan for Guided Reading
- Establishing the instructional focus

- Applying the focus strategy and other strategies

- Working with words

- Building fluency

After Reading Plan for Guided Reading
- Strategy follow-up activities

- Discussion Questions about the content of the text

- Questions for reflecting on the reading process

- Question for teaching written response to text

- Activity for connecting reading and writing through author's craft

PRE-READING PLAN FOR GUIDED READING

Prior knowledge questions to ask to get students ready to read:

Questions related to the topic/title/cover:

Ask: *Does the title or cover give us any clues about this text? What are the clues?*

Ask students questions related to background concepts they will need to understand this text such as:

How do people show that they really care about their work? (How could a teacher show that she cares about her job? A doctor? A student?)

Questions related to the genre:

Ask: *Is this text fiction or nonfiction? If it is fiction, is it a short story, drama, novel, poetry? How can you tell? What do you expect to find in this genre?*

Possible features of this text to highlight for students:

This is a poem. What do we expect to find in a poem?

Questions related to the author:

Ask: *Have you read anything else by this author? What? Based on other things you have read by this author, what do you expect this [story/chapter, etc.] to be like?*

Possible connections to make:

Someone named Ted Kooser wrote this poem. I don't think we've ever read anything by this author before, so this doesn't help us predict what this poem will be like.

Predictions to encourage:

Ask: (for fiction) *What do you think will happen in this [story/chapter, etc.]?* (for nonfiction) *What do you expect to learn?*

Possible predictions to make:

Students should predict that this poem will probably be about a woman named Myrtle with a passion for her work, since that is the theme we are investigating.

Purpose to establish:

Ask: *What do you hope to find out as you read this [story/ chapter, etc.]?*

Possible purposes to suggest:

Students should suggest that they will read this poem to find out about Myrtle's special passion, and how she showed this.

Vocabulary to teach:

1. Choose six to eight important words from the reading selection. (No more than four unknown words should be presented at one time.)
2. Create a word splash with these words.
3. Ask students how they predict each word will connect to the reading.
4. Provide instruction for any words that students do not understand.
5. Optional: Ask students to <u>write</u> sentences explaining how each word will connect to the reading.

Write new vocabulary words here:

slicker   pride   flicker   extinguish

Other words to include in Word Splash:

journal   porch   plastic   beaded

DURING READING PLAN FOR GUIDED READING

Establishing the instructional focus

Select <u>one</u> focus from <u>one</u> of the categories below:

Applying comprehension strategies to literary elements (fiction):

<u>Character Development</u>   Problem/theme/conflict   Plot/Events   Setting   Author's craft

Strategy focus lesson: <u>Notice what a character does or says or thinks to provide clues to the things that are important to him or her.</u>

Applying comprehension strategies to informational text (nonfiction):

Strategy focus lesson: _____

Applying the focus strategy and other strategies

Note some places in the reading selection where you want to model or prompt the use of the focus strategy to students:

> Has come through rain or darkness to bring us the news
> Likes a long walk in the morning
> Wrapped the news neatly in plastic
> Flickers from porch to porch
> Wind or weather can't extinguish her efforts

Note some places in the reading selection where you want to model or prompt the use of *other* strategies to students:

> Picture the woman wearing the yellow slicker
> Wonder who is watching her three small children when she's out delivering her papers
> Picture the paper wrapped in the WONDER Bread wrapper
> Connecting to the person who delivers my newspaper; I don't think she cares about her job as much (she just throws the paper anywhere.)
> Guessing that Myrtle might have another job during the day
> Notice that the author has compared Myrtle to a "yellow candle flame that no one can extinguish"
> Figuring out why the author compares Myrtle to a "yellow candle flame"

Working with words

Select some words you want to highlight for students to study. Why are you studying these particular words?

> Look at words that contain the "ea" vowel pattern. Sort them by vowel sound. Note the different sounds that /ea/ can make. Can you find other words to add to any of your /ea/sound lists?
>
> wearing   early   neatly   bread   beaded   reads   weather

Building fluency

Identify some good passages in this reading selection for students to practice their phrasing and expression during oral reading:

> Select one sentence that you especially like. Practice reading it with the kind of expression and phrasing that you think helps to convey its meaning. Be ready to read your sentence out loud the next time our group meets.

AFTER READING PLAN FOR GUIDED READING

Strategy Follow-up Activities:

Character Study

Discussion questions about the content of the text:

Constructing basic meaning:

Choose one word that best describes Myrtle and provide evidence from the poem to support your choice.

Think of another good title for this poem. Why would this be a good title?

Analyzing the text:

Why does the author compare Myrtle to a "yellow candle flame?"

Why do you think the author said "WONDER Bread bag" instead of just "bread bag?"

Text plus:

Do you think that Snowflake Bentley and Myrtle would have liked each other? Explain.

What do you think Myrtle might have written in her journal after returning home from her paper route?

Questions for reflecting on the reading process:

What strategy did we focus on today?
Did it help you understand this story better? In what way did it help?
Could you use this strategy in your own reading? Explain.

Question for written response to text:

Choose one word that best describes Myrtle and provide evidence from the poem to support your choice.

Connecting reading and writing through author's craft:

In this poem, the author creates a great "snapshot" of Myrtle so we can really picture her. What words and phrases does the author use to create this snapshot? How many senses does the author use to create this snapshot?

Create a snapshot of someone with a passion for his or her work. How many senses can you use to create your snapshot?

MULTI-DAY GUIDED READING PLANNER:
Supporting Students *Before*, *During*, and *After* Reading at their <u>Instructional</u> Level
(Template Cover Sheet)

Text: _____   Genre: _____

This text is part of a: ___Genre study   ___Author study   ___Theme study

Title of study: _____

This packet contains:

Pre-reading Plan for Guided Reading
• Prior knowledge questions to ask to get students ready to read

• Predictions to encourage

• Purpose to establish

• Vocabulary to teach

During Reading Plan for Guided Reading
• Establishing the instructional focus

• Applying the focus strategy and other strategies

• Working with words

• Building fluency

After Reading Plan for Guided Reading
• Strategy follow-up activities

• Discussion questions about the content of the text

• Questions for reflecting on the reading process

• Question for teaching written response to text

• Activity for connecting reading and writing through author's craft

PRE-READING PLAN FOR GUIDED READING

(Template)

Prior knowledge questions to ask to get students ready to read:

Questions related to the topic/title/cover:

Ask: *Does the title or cover give us any clues about this text? What are the clues?*
Ask students questions related to background concepts they will need to understand this text such as:

Questions related to the genre:

Ask: *Is this text fiction or nonfiction? If it is fiction, is it a short story, drama, novel, poetry? How can you tell? What do you expect to find in this genre?*
Possible features of this text to highlight for students:

Questions related to the author:

Ask: *Have you read anything else by this author? What? Based on other things you have read by this author, what do you expect this [story/chapter, etc.] to be like?*
Possible connections to make:

Predictions to encourage:

Ask: (for fiction) *What do you think will happen in this [story/chapter, etc.]?* (for nonfiction) *What do you expect to learn?*
Possible predictions to make:

Purpose to establish:

Ask: *What do you hope to find out as you read this [story/ chapter, etc.]?*
Possible purposes to suggest:

Vocabulary to teach:

1. Choose six to eight important words from the reading selection. (No more than four unknown words should be presented at one time.)
2. Write the words on a white board, chalk board, or transparency.
3. Ask students how they predict each word will connect to the reading.
4. Provide instruction for any words that students do not understand.
5. Optional: Ask students to <u>write</u> sentences explaining how each word will connect to the reading.

Write new vocabulary words here:

Other known words important to the text:

DURING READING PLAN FOR GUIDED READING

(Template)

Establishing the instructional focus

Select <u>one</u> focus from <u>one</u> of the categories below:

Applying comprehension strategies to literary elements (fiction):

    Character Development   Problem/theme/conflict   Plot/Events   Setting   Author's craft

    Strategy focus lesson: _____

Applying comprehension strategies to informational text (nonfiction):

    Strategy focus lesson: _____

Applying the focus strategy and other strategies

    Note some places in the reading selection where you want to model or prompt the use of the focus strategy for students:

    Note some places in the reading selection where you want to model or prompt the use of *other* strategies for students:

Working with words

Select some words you want to highlight for students to study. Why are you studying these particular words?

Building fluency

Identify some good passages in this reading selection for students to practice their phrasing and expression during oral reading:

AFTER READING PLAN FOR GUIDED READING

(Template)

Strategy Follow-up Activities:

Discussion Questions about the Content of the Text:
Constructing basic meaning:

Analyzing the text:

Text plus:

Questions for reflecting on the reading process:

Question for written response to text:

Activity for connecting reading and writing through author's craft:

8

Assessing Students' Reading Comprehension and Comprehension Strategy Use

⚙ Use multiple assessment measures, including oral and written measures, to monitor students' reading comprehension and their proficiency using comprehension strategies.

⚙ Ask students questions within different strands of thinking — constructing basic meaning (literal thinking), interpreting text (inferential thinking), and critical stance (evaluating and applying textual information) — to determine the depth of their understanding of what they read.

⚙ Use rubrics with clear criteria to determine how well your students can apply reading comprehension strategies to the texts they have read.

⚙ The rubrics included in this chapter will help you to measure the following:
  • Student competence applying individual comprehension strategies,
  • Student competence integrating these strategies to understand text, and
  • Student ability to respond, both orally and in writing, to comprehension questions about text.

How can you know whether your comprehension strategy instruction has improved your students' ability to understand what they read?

You might ask yourself whether, after reading, your students can construct basic meaning, whether they can interpret the text they have read, and whether they use their knowledge of the text to think critically and creatively.

Every reading teacher would like to be able to truthfully answer these questions affirmatively and with certainty. But how do you determine whether your students have achieved these goals or if they are even moving towards success with these goals?

Assessing Proficiency Using Comprehension Strategies

Students' Free Responses

Your students' oral reflections during whole-class shared reading sessions and teacher-guided small-group practice sessions offer abundant opportunity for an authentic assessment of their proficiency using comprehension strategies. In these settings, students' responses can give you an immediate glimpse of how well they can use these strategies, such as when a student chooses a strategy cue-card in a small-group session, or when a student tells the class about a connection he's made to the text, or discusses with the members of a small group how he noticed details in the text that led him to discover a theme.

Teacher-guided small-group sessions, especially, are a valuable occasion for you to monitor student interactions with text. Your students' free responses during such sessions can help you answer such questions as the following:

- How well can my students use individual comprehension strategies?

- How deeply have my students understood the text they have read?

- What do my students know about the process of negotiating meaning within a group?

Teacher Prompting for Improved Student Applications of Comprehension Strategies

When students willingly describe their use of comprehension strategies without any prompting from the teacher, you know they are applying these strategies automatically to understand what they read while they read. But if your students are reluctant to discuss their use of comprehension strategies, you may need to point out for them places in the text where they can apply these strategies to build a more thorough meaning from what they read. Your promptings will result in their enhanced oral reflections and will also help them to develop the habit of applying comprehension strategies to text that they might otherwise stumble over or misinterpret.

Here's a memorable example from a small-group teaching experience that helped me to understand the value of careful teacher-prompting of student use of these strategies. Seven fourth graders and I were sitting on a rug in the classroom's library corner, reading a poem by Jack Prelutsky, "Belinda Blue." We were focusing on using the strategy *wondering,* specifically, wondering why a character behaves a certain way. These students did a nice job of speculating about the answer to that question as they read about Belinda's tantrum when she was asked to eat "just one green bean." The students also offered rich visual images *picturing* Belinda's antics.

But there were some challenging words in this text. And while I was monitoring these students' abilities to apply comprehension strategies to the details of characterization, I also wondered whether they might be able to use comprehension strategies to understand new vocabulary. So, even though none of the students in this group had mentioned any words they didn't understand in the poem, I pointed to the final two lines of the first stanza.

> "I am livid!" she exploded.
> "I am bilious to the core!"

Then I asked, "Did anyone *notice* any difficult words in these lines, words that might get in the way of understanding this poem?"

Once I had prompted the students to look a little more closely at these last two lines, where, I suspected, they may not be able to understand all the words they saw there, they quickly identified two words that they did not know, *livid* and *bilious*. Once they had *noticed* the challenging words, we talked about strategies we might use to construct the correct meanings of these words. I suggested that we *notice* context clues to try to understand the meanings of these two words.

"I think these words mean that Belinda was really, really angry," offered Matt, almost whispering his response. His big brown eyes peeked out from under too-long wisps of blond hair, searching, it seemed, for affirmation.

"I think I agree with you," I volunteered. "Can you explain how you came to this conclusion?"

Matt was a kid who didn't often take a risk, so I wanted him to know right away that he was in safe territory. With more confidence now, he continued. "I looked at the lines right above these lines," he said. "And then I looked at the next line."

This was a perfect opportunity to show students in this small group how important it is to go back to text to validate your point of view. So I encouraged Matt to continue. "OK," I said. "Could you read those lines to us and show us exactly which words helped you?"

"Well," Matt said, "in the lines before *livid* and *bilious* it says, 'She beat her fist against the wall, she pounded on the floor.'"

Then Matt looked up at us. "Beating her fist and pounding on the floor…That's what a really angry person would do," he told us. "And the very next line says, 'She wrung her hands, she tore her hair.' Like I said, more angry stuff," he said, settling back into his chair, obviously satisfied that he'd done a fine job of explaining all of this to everyone in our group.

Matt was right. His discussion of how he guessed the meaning of the words from the lines around the words reinforced the strategies we had been discussing in this group for determining meaning from context. I wanted to celebrate his careful noticing, not only to reinforce the application of this strategy, but to acknowledge the contribution Matt had made to the group's understanding of the poem.

"I think Matt was so smart to check the sentences *above* the difficult words and also *after* the difficult words to see if he could figure out their meanings," I said. "I wonder how many of you will think to do that the next time you read a word that you don't understand?"

My challenge was more of a statement than a question. I wanted the kids to recognize the value of noticing how all the details in text can lead to improved comprehension. The difficult words in the poem, "Belinda Blue," provided an opportunity for me to prompt the students in the small group to apply comprehension strategies to build meaning for vocabulary that they might not otherwise understand.

Teacher prompting can also help students learn to apply a range of comprehension strategies to gain a more thorough understanding of text in many other ways, too. And I often find myself teasing meaning from young readers, sometimes just a few syllables at a time. The example of teacher prompting that follows is from my work with a sixth-grade small group, which was reading a passage from one of my all-time favorite books, *Mick Harte was Here* by Barbara Park.

After the students read the passage that described the father's pain upon entering his deceased son's room for the first time since the boy's bike accident, I asked the students, "Did anyone get a good picture of this scene?"

"I did," announced Darius right away.

"What did you picture?" I nudged. Anyone can *say* he has a picture in his mind. But I wanted detailed evidence of Darius's use of the picturing strategy.

"I pictured the father putting his hand on the doorknob and Mick's sister telling him not to go in there," he said.

"Yes," I said. "That's just what the book says. But if you were making a movie of this scene, how would the father look as he approached the door? How would Mick's sister sound as she begged her dad not to enter Mick's room?"

My goal in this kind of prompting was not to lead Darius to *my* interpretation of this passage, but to point out that quality visualizing requires more than simply parroting back the author's exact words. Quality visualizing entails creating your own, personalized and detail-rich image of a scene from the text.

Sometimes teachers have to do more prompting than they'd like in order to jump-start their students' use of comprehension strategies. And the handy chart, "Prompting Strategic Thinking," on Page 135 (and on the CD in the file titled, "EightA,") offers many and varied prompts to elicit a greater depth of thinking than your students might demonstrate in their free responses. For instance, to encourage self-monitoring of their understanding of the text while they read, you might ask, "At what points in the text did you stop reading to think about your comprehension so far? Why did you choose these stopping points?"

But good teachers will do more than prompt students' thinking about the text at hand. They will also encourage students to think ahead about how

Quality visualizing entails creating your own, personalized and detail-rich image of a scene from a text.

to apply comprehension strategies more independently the next time they read. "What will you do in the next chapter to keep track of your comprehension *before* meaning breaks down?" you might ask your students. These kinds of questions will help students be proactive rather than reactive.

Written Activities

Follow-up strategy activities can also help teachers monitor how well their students use comprehension strategies. You will find under "Comprehension Strategy Activities" (pages 154-197), several simple written activities you can use to assess student proficiency with each of the strategies. These activities are also included on the CD, in the files titled as follows: "EightB1," "EightB2," "EightB3," "EightB4," "EightB5," and "EightB6." These follow-up strategy activities encourage students to think one more time about their applications of specific strategies. Ask your students to complete one or two of these activities after each small-group reading lesson. You may also want them to use the follow-up strategy activity sheets to respond to shared reading or independent reading assignments.

The follow-up activities you will find in this book can best help you to document student progress using comprehension strategies — after oral discussion has taken place. Keep in mind that these written activities are not intended to take the place of oral discussion during the literacy block. Students get good at interpreting literature by talking about it. And that's natural. When we finish reading a book that we love (or a book that we find confusing or unsettling), we generally want to discuss it with others who have also read the book. A good book does not generally inspire its readers to fill out a sequence chart about the order of events or create a shoe-box display of a favorite scene. So while having students complete written follow-up activities can help a teacher to monitor student applications of comprehension strategies, these activities best gauge student comprehension only after the students have had sufficient opportunity to develop their thinking through oral response.

Assessing Comprehension of Text

Beyond assessing how well your students apply comprehension strategies, you will also want to know whether and to what extent their applications of these strategies helped them to understand what they read. Have they put the comprehension strategies you've offered them to good use? Have they used the strategies effectively to arrive at a deeper understanding of the reading selection?

Oral Responses to Comprehension Questions

Your first means for assessing students' comprehension of what they read must be their oral responses to your questions. Oral response allows even young children to respond to questions beyond the literal level, interpreting text and applying knowledge critically and creatively. Never forget that if *we,* as teachers, don't have high expectations of our students, they are not likely to achieve high standards. So while younger children may not think as abstractly as older readers, if we provide opportunities for even our younger readers to stretch their thinking during oral discussion, it is likely they will offer some truly brilliant insights. An oral format is also good for young readers because it allows them to hear their own thinking and to recognize when their spoken words fail to represent the thoughts in their head, thoughts that are often elaborate.

Once when I was working with a group of second graders, I asked them, when they had finished acting out a short skit based on the fairy tale, *Cinderella*, "Do you think there's a lesson we can learn from *Cinderella*?"

"Beauty!" declared Monique. Monique was one of those kids who always seemed to come up with the right answer right away, so I wondered if she'd even feel the need to rethink her response. But she did. She paused and looked thoughtful for several seconds before she continued. "What I mean," she said, "is that . . . beauty isn't just about your *outside* self. It's also about your inside self. Remember when Cinderella went back to looking like a maid? And the prince still loved her! He loved her *inner* beauty."

Monique's answer wasn't just a pretty good answer; it was a great answer! And I'm convinced that when Monique and other children hear their own responses in oral discussion, they know when they have or have not yet put all of what they are thinking into words. Monique heard her first answer, one spoken word, "beauty," and knew it didn't adequately reflect the thought she was trying to convey about the message of *Cinderella*. Would Monique have rethought her first answer if she'd already put it in writing, on paper, without the benefit of an oral rehearsal? How many one-word answers to thoughtful questions do *you* find on student papers?

Students' oral responses to questions about what they read also provide opportunities to celebrate language and build vocabulary around the study of literature. "Did you hear how Jacob used the word *conflict* to describe the problem at the beginning of this story?"

"Actually, Joey, I don't think '*metacognitioning*' is a real word; we'll just have to say, '*thinking about our thinking.*'"

Your students' oral responses will allow you to determine to what extent they are thinking about their thinking — and so much more. You will discover the following:

- Whether they can provide an answer in a complete sentence;

- Whether they know how to begin an oral response;

- Whether they can find the right words to express what they are trying to say;

- Whether their response is organized and makes sense; and

- Whether their answer contains sufficient details and evidence from the text to support their point of view.

I encourage teachers to plan text discussions around six open-ended comprehension questions — two from each thinking strand: constructing basic meaning, analyzing the text, and thinking beyond the text. On page 138, my chart, "Questions for Oral and Written Response to Text" (also included on the CD in the file titled, "EightD,"), offers several generic questions within the three thinking strands, questions that work well for both oral and written response to text. These questions will help your students reflect on what they have read *after* reading. Depending whether your focus is on literary analysis or on the comprehension strategies themselves, you may also want to use the two charts that follow on pages 140 and 142 and on the CD in the file "EightD," "Questions for Oral and Written Response Cross-Referenced to Analysis of Literary Elements," and "Questions for Oral and Written Response Cross-Referenced to Specific Comprehension Strategies."

When you apply these questions to what your students have read, you may find that they become so engrossed in the first question you ask, they are still debating the pros and cons of various perspectives twenty minutes later. You may not get to all of your questions. Don't worry! A focused conversation that probes deeply is more beneficial for your students than covering all of your questions in a superficial manner.

Written Answers

Comprehension assessment is not complete until students have represented their thinking about text in *writing*. Can your students produce accurate, organized, thorough, and fluent written answers to open-ended comprehension questions? These are the standards by which comprehension typically is measured on state achievement tests. Hence, we are doing our students a disservice if our literacy instruction stops short of helping them achieve the goal of quality written response to text.

Can your students produce accurate, organized, thorough, and fluent written answers?

While answering comprehension questions in writing *is* important, sometimes teachers go overboard in this area. I've visited too many classrooms where "reading instruction" is synonymous with lengthy packets containing page after page of questions that students must answer in writing and hand in for a grade. In this case, teachers shouldn't be surprised when children scribble down just enough words to get by. A better plan is to select one question and explicitly *teach* students how to respond to it in writing. That way, you celebrate quality, not quantity.

Rubrics for Assessing Students' Comprehension of Text and of the Reading Process

The comprehension strategies themselves, and questions related to understanding both the text and the reading process, define some of the *criteria* by which we can assess students' literacy performance. But how will we know how well readers are measuring up against these criteria? Rubrics can help.

Rubrics rely on a performance scale to identify students' strengths and weaknesses in regards to specific criteria. The rubrics I've included below use a simple "zero-to-two" range. Students performing at the top of the range (excellent) on a particular criteria would receive a score of two (2). Students at the next level (developing) would be awarded a one (1), and students deemed to be deficient would receive a zero (0).

Examining students' work analytically based on specific criteria and standards makes it possible for teachers to use assessment diagnostically to drive instruction.

Rubric for Assessing Students' Use of Integrated Strategies
Some students already use strategies consistently and well in both oral and written response. They activate different strategies depending on the nature of the text. You can easily find a clear, direct link between their use of strategies and their understanding of characters, plot, and other elements of the texts they read. They're eager to talk about how they are using strategies, and that strategy-talk sometimes even finds its way into curriculum areas beyond literacy.

Other students use strategies only superficially and may rely on a couple of favorites — like connecting and picturing. You usually need to prompt these students to describe their thinking, and their general level of comprehension remains mediocre.

Listen and watch closely as students practice the integrated use of all of their comprehension strategies during shared, guided, and independent reading. A teacher who monitors students' performance carefully will recognize strategy strengths and weaknesses and can plan future lessons to meet those needs. On page 144 the "Rubric for Assessing Students' Use of Integrated Strategies" (also included on the CD in the file titled, "Rubrics,") specifies some of the criteria teachers should keep in mind when monitoring and assessing students' use of blended comprehension strategies.

Rubric for Assessing Students' Use of an Individual Strategy
You will find guidelines to assess students' accurate use of each comprehension strategy in the "Rubric for Assessing Students' Use of an Individual Strategy" (available on page 145 and on the CD, in the file titled, "Rubrics,"). This rubric is particularly helpful in assessing the progress of readers following strategy-application focus lessons for fiction or informational text. As students reflect orally on text during guided reading, their levels of competence with individual strategies will become evident. Their competence in use of individual strategies can also be measured by students' performance on written strategy follow-up activities.

Rubric for Oral and Written Responses to Comprehension Questions

It is unlikely that *any* child could produce an accurate answer, whether written or spoken, to a question about a text that he or she truly does not understand. On the other hand, insufficient comprehension of text is not the only reason some students are unable to compose in writing an organized and thorough response to a comprehension question. A student may understand a text he has read and be able to respond well orally to questions about the text. But he will not be able, in written response, to express his understanding of the text if he is unfamiliar with the genre of written response. (To address this issue at length, see my book *Teaching Written Response to Text: Writing Quality Answers to Open-ended Comprehension Questions* Maupin House, 2002). Extreme difficulties with written fluency typically signify problems with language conventions due to language differences, language delays, or a host of other reasons. Of course, student grade level must be taken into consideration. We can and should expect more precision, better organization, greater thoroughness, and increased clarity of thought from older students.

In using the "Rubric for Assessing Oral and Written Response to Comprehension Questions" (see page 149 and, on the CD, the file titled, "Rubrics,") teachers should examine students' oral and written responses over time. As you explicitly teach the genre of written response and students practice it, you should find improvement in their written answers. Keep in mind that what is important in gauging their responses is not only how well they produce a summary (or any question response) today, but how much their responses to your questions improve when you ask the same questions in the coming weeks or even months.

I encourage teachers to assess students' written responses analytically rather than holistically (that is, with a single score to represent the level of their performance). By charting performance in each of the four areas (accuracy, organization, thoroughness, fluency) it is easier to plan next steps in instruction. For example, if a student's problem in written response to text is basically poor organization, you could spend time talking about the logical sequencing of ideas and good paragraph development. After a few more lessons in responding to a particular question, you can then observe whether the student has grown in the way she organizes an answer.

The Challenge

Is your comprehension strategy instruction really helping you to create better readers? Some teachers believe that improved reading scores on state achievement tests give them a positive answer to that important question. But no one way of teaching comprehension can *guarantee* higher scores.

Teaching comprehension in the explicit way this resource recommends, however, does increase the likelihood that your students will reach higher standards on state tests (or any other assessment measure) because the practices described here are based on solid principles of research-based instruction. You can't expect a quick fix, but you *can* expect to see steady growth in students' capacity to comprehend if you are steadfast in teaching comprehension strategies thoughtfully within a comprehensive literacy curriculum.

Thoughtful teaching of comprehension strategies means, in great part, knowing how and when to support readers as they read. You will be well on your way to being a very good teacher of reading comprehension if you:
- Explain strategies in language that students can understand;
- Model your use of these strategies;
- Let students practice integrating the strategies as they read books at their reading level;
- Give them more support when they need it;
- Teach focused strategy lessons throughout your literacy block; and
- Regularly monitor students' reading progress with several assessment tools.

The best teachers of comprehension continuously ask themselves: "What can I do to teach comprehension better?" It's a question that we each will answer again and again as we refine the teaching process and learn new ways to teach the reader, as well as the reading.

Prompting Strategic Thinking

Connecting
- Does this text remind you of anything that ever happened to you or to anyone you know? Can you explain? (Text-to-self connection)
- Have you read another book that is like this one in any way? How is it the same? (Text-to-text connection)
- What do you know already (from your background knowledge) that can help you understand this text better?) (Text-to-background knowledge/schema connection)
- Is this book like real life in any way? How is it like real life? (Text-to-world connection)
- How did you think of the connection you first made to this text? (Unpack the process)
- How does your connection to this text help you to understand it? (Link strategic thinking to comprehension)

Picturing
- What picture do you get in your mind when you read this [paragraph]?
- What other senses can you use to get a good impression of the scene this text brings to your mind?
- Go beyond just the words on the page to describe the picture in your mind. What else would be in your picture?
- Now add some more details to that picture in your mind so I can get a better picture of it in my mind.
- Look at the picture on the page. What did the illustrator think of putting in his/her picture that wasn't in your picture? What did you put in your picture of this scene that the illustrator left out of his or her picture?
- What other words could the author have included here to give the reader a better sense of this same scene?
- How did you get this picture in your mind? What were the clues in the text that helped you the most to create this mental picture? (Unpack the process)
- How did the pictures in your mind help you to understand this text? (Link strategic thinking to comprehension)

Wondering
- What questions has this text answered so far?
- What are you still wondering about? (A question to ask during reading)
- Now that you've finished this reading, do you have any questions that are still "floating around" in your mind? If you do, what are those questions? (A question to ask after reading)
- Are you still confused about anything you read? If yes, what in the text is confusing to you?
- If you could ask this author one [or more] questions, what would you ask? Why do you want to know about the answers to these questions, which the author has not answered in this text?
- How did you come up with your question? What did you think about to come up with such a great question? (Unpack the process)
- How did wondering help you understand this text better? (Link strategic thinking to comprehension)

Noticing

Noticing important clues to meaning

- What words in this [sentence / line / paragraph, etc.] do you think are the most important? Why? (Importance at the word level)

- If you could pick only one [sentence / paragraph] on this page as the most important one, which would it be? Why is that one important to you? (Importance at the sentence or paragraph level)

- How can you tell that the author thinks _____ is really important? Find proof in the text to support your answer. (Supporting opinions with evidence)

- What kind of author's craft is the author using here to make the writing lively? How could you use this craft in your own writing? (Noticing the reading-writing connection)

- Did you notice any words in this sentence that might be hard to say or understand and might get in the way of your comprehension of the text? (Monitoring for meaning)

- What is the most important idea you've gotten from this text? Why did you choose this idea? (Importance at the idea level)

- How did you "zero-in" on the words, sentences or ideas that seem most important? (Unpack the process)

- How did noticing important clues in the text help you to understand this text better? (Link the strategy of noticing to comprehension)

Noticing when meaning breaks down

- How will you decide where to pause as you read this text to check your understanding?

- Do you think you should pause often in this text to check your understanding? Or is this the kind of text in which you only need to pause occasionally to check your understanding of what you are reading?

- Support your answer with your own reasons or examples from the text of why this text is easy or hard to understand.

- How do you know when you're confused during your reading? What signs tell you that you have lost the meaning of the text?

- When you're trying to fix your comprehension, how do you decide which of your other comprehension strategies might be the most helpful?

- How can you tell when your thinking is back on track with the meaning of the text?

Figuring Out (Inferring)

- What do you think will happen in this story? What do you think will happen next? How do you think this story will end? (Using prediction in a narrative text)

- What do you expect to learn from this text? (Using prediction in informational text)

- The author is showing us something here rather than telling us directly. What do you think the author wants us to know, to be able to figure out for ourselves? (Using inference to draw conclusions)

- What caused _____ to happen? Although the author doesn't tell us directly, we can figure out for ourselves what caused that to happen. (Using inference to see cause-and- effect relationships)

- Do you think the author is trying to teach us a lesson (or send us a message) through this text? What is it? Why do you think that is the message the author is sending the readers in this text? (Using inference to determine theme)

- How did you come up with that great inference? What information in the text helped you? (Unpack the process)

- How did your making predictions about what would happen next in the story help you to understand this story? (Link predictions to comprehension)
- How did your figuring out what the author is trying to show the readers help you to understand this text? (Link inference about theme or main idea to comprehension)

Figuring Out (Synthesis)
- In just a few sentences, describe this text as if you are discussing it with someone who has never read it. (Summarizing)
- If you were explaining this story to a younger child, how would you explain it? (Simplifying language, consolidating the text)
- At what point did you say to yourself, "Aha, now I get it!"? (Awareness of thinking process)
- What were the best clues in this text, the ones that really helped you figure out what was going on? (Using evidence to put the pieces together)
- What do you think might be on a test about this reading? (Distilling the most important points)
- Which strategies helped you to figure out the meaning of this text? (Recognizing that many strategies converge to help readers synthesize)
- Did this reading change or confirm what you thought about _____ ? Explain. (Synthesizing extends, changes, or reaffirms knowledge)
- How did you go about figuring this out? (Unpack the process of putting the pieces together)
- If a reader can't figure out how all the pieces of a text fit together, how would you help him/her to solve this problem? (Link synthesis with comprehension)

Questions for Oral and Written Response to Text

(For Narrative and Expository Text)

Questions on pages 138–143 are designated with Roman numerals and capital letters. The Roman numerals correspond to the three different strands of thinking. You will find the same numbering system for these questions if you are using my book, *Teaching Written Response to Text.*

I. Constructing Basic Meaning

    A. According to this text, [who / when / where / why / how] _____? Why is this detail important?

    B. Choose one word that best describes [name of character / person] and provide evidence from the text to support your choice.

    C. What is the problem or conflict in this text?

    D. Briefly summarize what happens in this story.

    E. How does [the main character / important person] solve his/her problem in this text?

    F. What was your first reaction to this [story / chapter / article]? Please explain using specific examples.

    G. What would you say is the main idea of this text?

    H. If you could rename this [story / article / chapter], what would you call it and why?

II. Analyzing the Text

    A. How did [character / person] change from the beginning of the text to the end of the text?

    B. What is the purpose of this [paragraph / line] on page ___?

    C. What details in the text support the conclusion that _____?

    D. What lesson can we learn from this [article / story / chapter]?

    E. Choose a [line / paragraph] from this text that you consider very important. Why do you think it is important?

    F. Do you consider this text to be "good literature"? Tell me why you feel it is good literature or why it is not good literature.

    G. What author's craft techniques used in this text make the writing lively? Give examples.

    H. From whose point of view is this text written? Why do you think the author chose this voice? Give examples from the reading to support your answer.

    I. What is the structure of this text? Why do you think the author chose this structure?

    J. Choose one fact and one opinion in this text. How do you know that one is a fact and the other is an opinion?

    K. How can you tell that the [character / person / author] cared about _____? Use information from the text to support your answer.

III. Text Plus

    A. How is this text similar to another text you read?

    B. What might [character / person] have written in his or her journal after this happened in the text?

    C. List ___ questions you would like to ask the author that are <u>not</u> answered in this text. Explain why you would like an answer to each of these still-unanswered questions.

    D. Based on information in this text, what would probably have happened if _____?

    E. Using information from the text, how do you visualize this scene?

    F. Does [something or someone] in this text remind you of [something or someone] in your own life? Explain or describe.

    G. If you had been [person / character], how would you have handled the situation when _____?

    H. How is [someone or something] described in this text similar to someone or something in our world today?

    I. What do you think will happen next? Use information from this text to support your answer.

    J. Imagine that you are giving a talk to your class about _____. Using information from the text, write two ideas you would use in this speech.

Questions for Oral and Written Response
Cross-Referenced to Analysis of Literary Elements

Character Study

I.A   Who was the most important character in this story, and why was this character important?

I.B   Choose one word that best describes the character and provide evidence from the text to support your choice.

I.E   How does the main character solve his/her problem in this story?

II.A   How did a particular character change from the beginning of the story to the end of the story?

II.K   How can you tell that a particular character cared about _____? Use information from the story to support your answer.

III.B   What might a particular character have written in his or her journal after a particular event happened in the story?

III.D   Based on what happened in this story, what might have been different if the character responded to this situation in another way?

III.F   Does someone in this story remind you of someone in your own life? Explain.

III.G   If you had been this character, how would you have handled the situation when _____?

III.H   How is someone in this story like someone in our world today?

Setting

I.A   What is the setting in this story? Why is this setting important?

III.D   Based on information in this story, what in this story may have been different if it had been set in a different place or time? What may have been the same if the story was set in a different place or time?

Problem/Conflict

I.A   In this story, why did this event occur?

I.C   What is the problem or conflict in this story? Give specific details to support your answer.

I.F   What was your first reaction to this story? Please explain using specific examples.

II.D   What lesson can we learn from this story?

III.E   Using information from the text, how do you visualize this scene?

Plot/Events

I.A   What happens in this part of the story and why is this event important?

I.D   Briefly summarize what happens in this story.

I.H   If you could rename this story, what would you call it and why?

II.B   What is the purpose of this [paragraph / line] on page _____?

II.C   What details in this story support the conclusion that _____?

II.E   Choose a line / paragraph from this text that you consider to be very important. Why do you think it is important?

III.D   Based on information in this story, what would probably have happened if _____?

III.E   Using information from this story, how do you visualize this scene?

III.I   What do you think will happen next? Use information from the story to support your answer.

Author's Craft

I.F   What was your first reaction to this story? Please explain using specific examples.

II.F   Do you consider this text to be "good" literature? Why or why not?

II.G   What are some of the author's-craft techniques used in this story that makes the writing lively? Give examples.

II.H   From whose point of view is this story written? Why do you think the author chose this voice? Give examples from the reading to support your answer.

II.I   What is the structure of this text? Why do you think the author chose this structure?

III.C   List _____ questions you would like to ask the author that are <u>not</u> answered in this text. Tell why you want an answer to each question.

Questions for Oral and Written Response
Cross-Referenced to Specific Comprehension Strategies

Connecting

I.F What was your first reaction to _____ ?

III.A How is this text similar to another text you read?

III.F Does someone or something in this text remind you of someone or something in your own life?

III.G If you had been [person], how would you have handled the situation when___?

III.H How is someone or something described in this text similar to someone or something in our world today?

Picturing

III.E Using information from the text, how do you visualize this scene? What other sensory details from

the text contribute to your impression of the scene?

Wondering

III.C List __ questions you would like to ask the author that are <u>not</u> answered in this text.

Predicting/Guessing

III.D Based on information in this text, what would probably have happened if___?

III.I What do you think will happen next? Use information from this text to support your answer.

Noticing

I.A According to this text, who/when/where/why/how ___?

I.C What is the problem in this text?

I.E How does the [main character / important person] solve his/her problem in this text?

II.A How did [character/person] change from the beginning of the text to the end of the text?

II.B What is the purpose of this [paragraph]?

II.C What details in the text support the conclusion that
_____?

II.G What author's-craft techniques used in this text make the writing lively? Give examples.

II.I What is the structure of this text?

Figuring Out

I.B   Choose one word that best describes [person] and provide evidence from the text supporting your choice of this word."

I.D   Briefly summarize what happens in this story.

I.G   What would you say is the main idea of this text?

I.H   If you could rename this [story / article / chapter], what would you call it and why?

II.D   What lesson can we learn from this [article / story / chapter]?

II.E   Choose a line that you consider to be very important. Why do you think it is important?

II.F   Do you consider this text to be "good literature"? Why or why not?

II.H   From whose point of view is this text written?

II.J   Choose one fact and one opinion in this text. How do you know that one is a fact and the other is an opinion?

II.K   How can you tell that the author or person in the text cared about _____?

III.B   What might [character / person] have written in his/her journal after this happened?

III.J   Imagine that you are giving a talk to your class about ____. Using information from the text, write two ideas you would use in this speech.

Rubric for Assessing Students' Use of Integrated Strategies

Criteria	2 Excellent	1 Developing	0 Deficient
Accurate use of strategies (See **Metacognitive Strategy Rubric** for criteria for each strategy.)	Uses comprehension strategies accurately almost all of the time to probe deep meaning of text	Generally uses comprehension strategies accurately. Strategies may sometimes be mislabeled or some strategy applications may be superficial	Strategy applications are often inaccurate and/or superficial
Flexible uses of strategies	Uses a varied repertoire of strategies and recognizes when a particular strategy could be especially helpful in constructing meaning	Tends to rely on a few "favorite" strategies and doesn't seem to see the relative merits of one strategy over another in particular reading situations	Seems to feel comfortable with only one or two strategies and relies on them even when they are not relevant
Uses strategies to construct meaning	A clear link is apparent between the student's use of comprehension strategies and their good comprehension of text, often with direct student reference to one or more strategies	Use of comprehension strategies sometimes results in improved comprehension, though this improvement generally occurs just within literal-level thinking about text.	Comprehension remains poor despite instructional focus on comprehension strategies
Actively engages in strategy use	Initiates use of strategies without prompting or modeling; actively uses strategies during group discussions and independent reading	Uses strategies willingly during group and independent work, but sometimes needs prompting	Seldom uses strategies without specific teacher-prompting or modeling

Rubric for Assessing Students' Use of an Individual Strategy

Strategy	2 Excellent Strategy Application	1 Developing Strategy Application	0 Superficial or Nonexistent Strategy Application
Connecting	"I once fell off my bike, just like the character in this story. I know how he felt, not wanting to get on his bike again, because that was how I felt after my fall. I bet he feels nervous, just like I did." (This kind of connection makes it clear that the student's experience is helping him connect to the emotions of the character.)	"I once fell off my bike, just like the character in this story." (This connection might be a good one, but it's hard to tell because the student offers no elaboration. You would need to probe: "How does that experience — falling off your bike — help you to understand this story?")	"In the story, the dog's name is Shep, and my friend has a dog named Shep." (Superficial connection)
Picturing	"I can picture the dog. Her long, floppy ears are hanging in her water dish as she laps her water noisily. Her brown-and-white fur is all matted and she smells bad because she was left outside too long by her former owner, and she didn't get any baths." (The student uses the clues provided by the author, but goes beyond the words on the page to personalize the image with details that can be inferred.) (Frequent, unprompted references to various senses)	"I can picture the dog. The author says she has long, floppy ears, and she is white with brown spots." (The student is providing details exactly as they are stated in the text. The student is mostly retelling; references other senses only when prompted.)	"I've got a good picture of this scene in my mind." "I can really picture the dog in this story." (No details are offered; There are no references to any other senses.)

Rubric for Assessing Students' Use of an Individual Strategy

Strategy	2 Excellent Strategy Application	1 Developing Strategy Application	0 Superficial or Nonexistent Strategy Application
Wondering	"Why do you think *The Giving Tree* kept giving to the boy even when the boy never gave anything in return?" "Should people just give and give, even when someone treats them unkindly?" (These questions address theme and extend students' thinking beyond the text itself.)	"I wonder what will happen next?" (This is a reasonable question because we want students to remain curious about the outcome of the story. That's what keeps them reading. But we also want them to dig deeper.)	"Why is the girl in the story wearing a blue sweater?" (This question has no real relationship to the story. The student is probably asking this question because he is focusing on the illustrations, rather than on the text.)
Guessing (Predicting)	"I'm guessing that the thing that will happen next in this story is _____ because _____ and _____ ." (The student clearly bases predictions on multiple sources of evidence from the text.)	"I'm guessing that the thing that will happen next in this story is _____ because the event right before this was _____." (The student uses evidence to make a prediction, but doesn't consider multiple sources.)	"I have no idea what will happen next." Or the student's prediction has no connection to text evidence. (The student does not engage actively enough with the text to even make a prediction, or the prediction is completely random.)

Rubric for Assessing Students' Use of an Individual Strategy

Strategy	2 Excellent Strategy Application	1 Developing Strategy Application	0 Superficial or Nonexistent Strategy Application
Noticing the Important Parts	"I noticed that the author is giving lots of clues about what this character is like. I am learning about this character by his actions, his words, his thoughts, and the way he looks." (The student uses the important clues she finds about a character as a springboard to understanding this character.)	"I noticed that on this page the author is letting us know who the main character is." (This student identified an essential story component, which will contribute to synthesis later on.)	The student uses his yellow highlighter to highlight everything on the page or nothing on the page. (This student is having a tough time separating important from unimportant information.)
Noticing When Comprehension Breaks Down	"I see a word I don't understand, 'tundra.' How could I figure out what this word means? Oh, there's a glossary in the back of this book!" (The student not only notices right away when comprehension breaks down, but also is a problem-solver.)	"On the second page, I found a word I don't understand: tundra. I think I'll reread that page." (The student recognizes when her or his comprehension breaks down and attempts to reread portions of the text, or reads ahead. However, the student expects comprehension to be improved only by rereading; there are no other thinking strategies applied at the point of difficulty to foster improved understanding.)	The student reads right through to the end of the text without realizing he is having trouble comprehending what he is reading.

Rubric for Assessing Students' Use of an Individual Strategy

Strategy	2 Excellent Strategy Application	1 Developing Strategy Application	0 Superficial or Nonexistent Strategy Application
Figuring Out (Inferring)	"I think that that the author's message from *The Three Little Pigs* is that work should come before play. It was all that playing that got the first two little pigs into trouble." (The student determines not only the lesson, but draws upon text evidence to support the inference.)	"I think the author's message is that wolves are mean." (The student does understand the role of character traits in the story, but misses cause-and-effect relationships.)	No idea what the author's message might be. Or, "The author doesn't like hay." (The student determines a message that is very concrete and tied to an incidental detail in the text.)
Figuring Out (Synthesizing)	"In this poem the author says the animal is scary, has big feet and a long neck, and lives in Asia on prairies. At first I thought it was a giraffe because I was just concentrating on the clue about the long neck. But then I read the line about the hump on its back, so I figured out it was probably a camel. All of the clues fit together to describe a camel, except I'm still wondering why the author said it was 'scary.' I disagree with that part. Also, I thought camels lived in the desert. I'll check that out." (The student identifies the significant details to arrive at a conclusion not stated in the text. She is aware of her thought processes and thinks critically about the content of what she has read. She merges new information with prior knowledge to expand her schema about camels.)	"In this poem the author says the animal has big feet and a long neck. It lives in Asia on the prairie, has a hump, and is a little scary. It is probably a camel." (The student provides a basic retelling or summary of the text, including most or all important details, and is able to put the clues together to draw a conclusion. The student is able to put thoughts into her or his own words, but there is no critical thinking about content.)	The student can't figure out how all the pieces fit together or can't identify main characters, the problem, setting, etc. "In this poem the author says the animal has a long neck, and big feet, and it has a 'beastly bump.'" (The student recalls fragments of text, sometimes using the author's exact words. There's no effort to tie ideas together or to convert thoughts to language that shows understanding.)

Rubric for Assessing Students' Oral and Written Response to Comprehension Questions

Criteria	2 Excellent	1 Developing	0 Deficient
Accuracy	The answer is completely accurate; The answer is clearly based on events in the text that really happened, correctly represents factual information, and formulates reasonable inferences.	The answer is partially accurate. The answer shows some confusion about events or information described in the text, and inferences may be "far-fetched" or not tied directly to the content of the reading.	The answer is clearly inaccurate and is well below the range of developmental level expectations. The answer does not indicate that the student has constructed basic meaning from the text, either explicitly stated information, or inferred relationships among ideas. The answer may point to problems that go deeper than comprehension, perhaps insufficient word identification skills.
Organization	The answer is logically organized. The answer follows the steps specified in the response criteria or uses another sequential structure that makes sense to the reader.	The answer is marginally organized. The answer may begin in a logical fashion, but loses its focus, or the parts may all be present, but are not well-sequenced.	The answer has no organizational framework and is well below the range of grade level expectations. The answer may be too sparse to provide a sense of organization, or it may be very long and repetitive, saying the same thing over and over in a variety of ways, or it may be largely incoherent with no sense of direction.
Thoroughness	The answer is thorough according to grade-level expectations. The answer meets all criteria for details and elaboration specified for the response to a particular question, and the details show a close, careful reading of the text.	The answer is more general than specific. The answer contains some details and elaboration, but the student has missed or has neglected to include enough evidence from the text to sufficiently support a general statement or main idea.	The answer is vague and/or irrelevant and is well below the range of grade level expectations. The answer may be so general, far-fetched, or so loosely tied to the text that it is hard to tell whether the student has even read the text.
Fluency	The answer flows smoothly. The answer demonstrates grade-level appropriate competence with grammar, usage, writing conventions, vocabulary, and language structure.	The answer sounds somewhat "choppy." The answer is generally able to be read and understood, but may show more carelessness or lack of proficiency in the use of grammar, usage, writing conventions, vocabulary, and language structure than is appropriate for a student at this grade level.	The answer is nearly incomprehensible because of written language deficits and is well below the range of grade-level expectations. It shows extreme lack of skill in communicating ideas in writing, and may signal the need for interventions beyond the scope of written response instructional supports.

Supporting Materials

Comprehension Strategy Activities

Annotated Bibliography of Children's Literature

Strategy Mini-Posters, Cue-Cards, and Bookmarks

Growing Professionally through the Study of Comprehension

Comprehension Strategy Activities

Activities for Applying Multiple Strategies

The following two pages are reproducible activity sheets. These activity sheets are also on the CD in the file titled, "ThreeB."

The Active Reader Report

This activity is an effective means for you to monitor students' proficiency with the full spectrum of cognitive strategies. This activity may be used in two ways. First, it may be used as a follow-up to a discussion about a text segment. In this case, children take the sheet back to their seats after the group has met and complete it in regards to the portion of text they just read. Another possibility that works well with students who are already strong strategy users is for them to complete this activity *before* the group session, answering the questions in regards to the text selection they have read independently. In the latter example, the responses students record in the Active Reader Report become the springboard for group conversation about the text.

Whichever way you choose to use this activity, be sure to model the way this sheet would be filled out before expecting students to do it themselves.

The Strategy Slip

Students find this an easy way to begin to monitor, through writing, their uses of comprehension strategies. This activity works well even with children in the primary grades. Students simply circle one strategy that they feel helped them to understand the day's text segment, and then they offer in writing one specific example from their reading where that strategy was useful. Returning to the text for actual evidence is a valuable habit students need to build beginning in the primary grades.

ACTIVE READER REPORT

Name: _____ Date: _____

Text title: _____ Pages: _____

One prediction I made was:	**Here's something I didn't understand:** **Here's what I did to try to solve my problem:**
As I read, I got a good picture of this in my mind:	**Here's something I figured out that the author didn't tell me:**
Here's a connection I made between something in the text and something in my own life or in another text:	**Something I'm still wondering about after reading this text is:**

STRATEGY SLIP

Name: _____   Date: _____

One strategy I used today to help me understand this text is:

       Connecting   **Wondering**   **Picturing**

       Guessing   **Noticing**   **Figuring out**

Here's a place in the text where I used this strategy: _____

_____

_____

_____

STRATEGY SLIP

Name: _____   Date: _____

One strategy I used today to help me understand this text is:

       Connecting   **Wondering**   **Picturing**

       Guessing   **Noticing**   **Figuring out**

Here's a place in the text where I used this strategy: _____

_____

_____

_____

     © 2004 Nancy N. Boyles, *Constructing Meaning*

Activities for Connecting

The following five pages are reproducible activity sheets. These activity sheets are also available on the CD in the file titled, "EightB1."

I Have a Connection
This is a good activity for students in the primary grades, students new to using strategies, or below-grade-level readers. This activity asks students to make any kind of connection and then draw a picture of their connection. The writing may be done by either the teacher or the student.

I'm Connected
Use this activity with students in the intermediate and upper-elementary grades (approximately grades 3 – 6). This activity not only encourages students to make various kinds of connections, but also asks them to think about how their connection influenced their understanding.

One Word
This is a good activity to use with older or more advanced readers. It provides students an opportunity to think a bit more abstractly about their connection, relating not just to the events of a text, but to the theme, as well.

Connecting to Time and Place
This follow-up activity encourages students to reflect on their perceptions about the setting of a text. Coming to terms with whether or not you would like to live in a particular time and place requires a deeper connection to the reading than simply recalling where a text is set.

Friends I Might Have Known
Would you like a specific character or person from history for your personal friend? Why or why not? This follow-up sheet asks students to consider those questions to derive some connections at a higher thinking level.

I HAVE A CONNECTION

Name: _____   Date: _____

Text: _____

Today I read about: _____

_____

_____

```


```

Here is my connection: _____

_____

_____

I'M CONNECTED

Name: _____   Date: _____

Text: _____

I can make a connection between something I read and:

    ✓ Something in my own life

    ✓ Something in another book

    ✓ Something in the world today

Here is what I read:

_____

_____

_____

Here is my connection:

_____

_____

_____

_____

Here is how my connection helped me understand this text better: _____

_____

_____

_____

_____

ONE WORD

Name: _____   Date: _____

Text: _____

Choose one word that you think **best** represents this text. Write it here:

_____

I chose this word because _____

_____

_____

A time when this word was important in my own life was when _____

_____

_____

_____

A time when this word was important in another text I read was when _____

_____

_____

_____

A time when this word had "real world" connection was when _____

_____

_____

CONNECTING TO TIME AND PLACE

Name: _____   Date: _____

Text: _____

The events in this text are set in this place: _____

at this time: _____

I would / would not like to live during this time and in this place because _____

_____

_____

_____

Here are some details from the reading that helped to convince me about this:

1._____

_____

2._____

_____

3._____

_____

FRIENDS I MIGHT HAVE KNOWN

Name: _____   Date: _____

Text: _____

Name of character or person: _____

I would / would not like _____

for a friend because _____

_____

_____

Here are some details from the reading that prove what I am saying:

1. _____

   _____

2. _____

   _____

3. _____

   _____

   _____

© 2004 Nancy N. Boyles, *Constructing Meaning*

Activities for Picturing
and for Imagining Other Sensory Impressions

The following five pages contain four reproducible activity sheets. These activity sheets are also available on the CD in the file titled, "EightB2."

Picture This

Even young children use this activity sheet successfully. The idea is to find a sentence in the text that brings a great mental image to mind. The student selects his or her own sentence and then draws a picture using plenty of details. Sometimes I choose the sentence if I am checking comprehension of a specific idea.

What's in a Picture?

This follow-up activity asks students to look closely at an illustration and also to think inferentially about it. By noticing the small details in a picture and reflecting on why the author may have included a particular graphic as well as what that graphic represents, readers will become more adept at "reading" the picture. They will better recognize how the picture contributes to their comprehension of the text as a whole.

Visualize Vocabulary

When students can verbalize word meanings, especially when they are able to translate meanings into their own words, we assume students understand them fairly well. But can the student draw a simple picture that represents the word? Illustrating vocabulary takes word study to another level: application. This activity sheet is useful for both literature study and informational texts. Some teachers using this activity have bound several of these activity pages together to create vocabulary books for their students as they study a novel or chapter in their social studies book.

Reading with All of my Senses

We want students to realize that creating mental images is about more than just *visual* imagery; it is about using *all* of their senses. This follow-up sheet helps to achieve that goal in a simple, direct manner. Note that in addition to the "usual" five senses, there is also the notion here of getting in touch with the emotional imagery that the text or picture evokes.

PICTURE THIS

Name: _____   Date: _____

Text: _____

```
┌─────────────────────────────────────────────────────────┐
│                                                           │
│                                                           │
│                                                           │
│                                                           │
│                                                           │
│                                                           │
│                                                           │
│                                                           │
│                                                           │
│                                                           │
│                                                           │
│                                                           │
│                                                           │
└─────────────────────────────────────────────────────────┘
```

I have a good picture of this sentence in my mind: _____

_____

_____

WHAT'S IN A PICTURE?

Name: _____   Date: _____

Text: _____

What kind of graphic is this (photo, chart, graph, map, cut-away, drawing, etc.)?

Find 3 or more details in this graphic that only careful observers would notice:

1. _____   4. _____

2. _____   5. _____

3. _____   6. _____

Circle one or more traits or feelings that you think this graphic represents:

Courage   Kindness   Friendliness   Fear   Happiness

Jealousy   Creativity   Love   Strength   Cleverness

Bravery   Discrimination   Hope   Determination   Pain

Joy   Compassion   Danger   Diversity   Pride

Beauty   Success   Frustration   Anger   Honesty

Contentment   Confusion   Other: _____

Why do you think the author included this picture?

_____

_____

VISUALIZE VOCABULARY

Name: _____   Date: _____

Text: _____

Please use these words from your reading to complete the activity below:

The word: _____

The meaning (in my own words): _____

_____

The picture in my mind:

The word: _____

The meaning (in my own words): _____

_____

The picture in my mind:

The word: _____

The meaning (in my own words): _____

_____

The picture in my mind:

The word: _____

The meaning (in my own words): _____

_____

The picture in my mind:

The word: _____

The meaning (in my own words): _____

_____

The picture in my mind:

READING WITH ALL OF MY SENSES

Name: _____   Date: _____

Text: _____

When I read this text or looked at this picture, here's what I experienced:

I saw _____ and it looked [like]

_____

I heard _____ and it sounded [like]

_____

I smelled _____ and it smelled [like]

_____

I tasted _____ and it tasted [like]

_____

I touched _____ and it felt [like]

_____

It touched my heart and I felt _____ because

_____

Activities for Questioning and Wondering

The following three pages are reproducible activity sheets. These activity sheets are also available on the CD in the file titled, "EightB3."

Questions. . . Questions. . . Questions

This activity sheet will help students understand the difference between questions that are answered in the text and questions that the text does not answer. This activity will introduce even younger students to this important distinction. As you assess your students' performance, help them differentiate between quality questions and those that are of little consequence to comprehension.

True or False

Kids really enjoy this activity! The basic idea is that they develop questions from text that can be answered with either "true" or "false." This is a good way to monitor whether students can construct basic meaning. They also enjoy trading questions with each other, which becomes another good way to check comprehension. Teachers should note that this questioning activity does not promote higher level thinking skills. For that, consider using *The Question is. . .* (See below)

The Question Is. . . .

This activity helps children to practice asking questions at different levels of thinking. To teach this concept I translate the language of questioning into terms more accessible to students new to the notion of leveled questions. (See this activity sheet for redefinition of terms.) Use of this activity sheet should follow careful teaching of the leveled questions concept.

QUESTIONS. . . . . QUESTIONS. . . . . .QUESTIONS

Name: _____   Date: _____

Text: _____

What are three questions that this text answers?

   1. _____

   2. _____

   3. _____

What questions do I still have after doing this reading that are *not* answered right in the text? (Try to think of three questions.)

   1. _____

   2. _____

   3. _____

TRUE OR FALSE

Name: _____   Date: _____

Text: _____

Write as many questions as you can about this text for which the answer is either *true* or *false*.

1. _____

2. _____

3. _____

4. _____

5. _____

6. _____

7. _____

8. _____

9. _____

10. _____

THE QUESTION IS . . . .

Name: _____   Date: _____

Text: _____

Computer question:
Write a question that can be answered with information stated directly in this text.

_____

_____

Detective question:
Write a question that you can figure out from reading this text, even though the author doesn't tell you the information directly.

_____

_____

Judge question:
Write a question that you can answer by combining information from the text with information already in your mind in order to make a decision or form an opinion.

_____

_____

Inventor question:
Write a question that you can answer by combining information from the text with information already in your mind in order to develop a plan or create something.

_____

_____

Activities for Noticing
(Determining Important Clues)

The following three pages are reproducible activity sheets. These activity sheets are also available on the CD in the file titled, "EightB4."

Prove it!

This activity (also included in *Teaching Written Response to Text*, Maupin House, 2002) can be used with students of almost any age (except for the very young!). It reinforces the need to support responses to open-ended questions with specific evidence from the text.

The teacher should fill in the page number and the first blank line (the idea that needs to be "proven.") The teacher should also teach students the proper format for citing evidence in the author's own words, including punctuating sentences with quotation marks. This activity sheet works well with both fiction and informational text.

"Best Quote"

This activity offers students practice in identifying parts of a text that they feel are important. Students need to read carefully to decide what kind of information the author is providing, as well as why the information is significant to the story (for fiction) and main idea (in informational text).

Mirror, Mirror. . .

Students can complete this activity in two phases, first individually, and then in cooperative groups. I usually specify the number of words that students must identify (between 5 and 10). As they read, they are instructed to look for and write down the words that they feel are the most important. Rather than providing a definition of the word, they must indicate why they have selected a particular word, which requires more critical thinking than simply copying information out of a glossary or dictionary.

After students have completed this activity individually, they meet with a group of four or five other students to compile a single list of the required number of words. This is where it gets interesting because students have to defend their choices and convince other group members that their word(s) belong on the master list. Expect animated discussion. Even middle school students enjoy this activity, which works especially well with informational text.

PROVE IT!

Name: _____   Date: _____

Text: _____

1. Read page _____ and find a sentence that proves that _____

   _____

   Proof: _____

   _____

   _____

2. Read page _____ and find a sentence that proves that _____

   _____

   Proof: _____

   _____

   _____

3. Read page _____ and find a sentence that proves that _____

   _____

   Proof: _____

   _____

   _____

© 2004 Nancy N. Boyles, *Constructing Meaning*

"BEST QUOTE"

Name: _____ Date: _____

Text: _____

Find a quote from this text that seems very important. It can be important for any reason.

What is the page number? _____

Write the quote here: (Remember quotation marks.)

_____

_____

_____

_____

Why do you think this quote is important?

_____

_____

_____

_____

MIRROR, MIRROR ON THE WALL,
WHAT ARE THE MOST IMPORTANT WORDS OF ALL?

Name: _____   Date: _____

Text: _____

Find _____ words

Word   Reason

1. _____   _____

2. _____   _____

3. _____   _____

4. _____   _____

5. _____   _____

6. _____   _____

7. _____   _____

8. _____   _____

9. _____   _____

10. _____   _____

Activities for Noticing
(Monitoring Meaning)

The following three pages are reproducible activity sheets. These activity sheets are also available on the CD in the file titled, "EightB4."

Clued In

This activity encourages students to monitor the meaning they are building while they read. The activity helps them to develop awareness of the clues the author is providing so they can figure out something important about the text. It's a good activity to use after the entire text has been read. Students would need to reflect on their reading to determine which clues (or evidence) led them to a particular conclusion.

Stuck and Unstuck

This activity helps students recognize when they are stuck during their reading and helps them to learn to problem-solve to get their thinking back on track. Even young children can monitor their comprehension in this way and learn to apply strategies to fix-up their understanding while they are reading.

Stop and Think

One of the most difficult aspects of monitoring is deciding on appropriate places to stop and think about the reading you've done so far. This activity gives students practice in making that important decision to pause and reflect. Developing this competence is essential to independent reading.

CLUED IN

Name: _____   Date: _____

Text: _____

1. The author included these clues:

    a. _____

    b. _____

    c._____

    to help me figure out: _____

    _____

    _____

2. The author included these clues:

    a. _____

    b. _____

    c._____

    to help me figure out: _____

    _____

    _____

STUCK AND UNSTUCK

Name: _____   Date: _____

Text: _____

Here is something I read that confused me: _____

_____

_____

I used this strategy (or strategies) to help me fix up my comprehension:

    Rereading   Connecting   Visualizing   Questioning

        Inferring   Synthesizing   Finding the important clues

    Some other strategy: _____

Here is how I used this strategy to help me: _____

_____

_____

_____

STOP AND THINK

Name: _____   Date: _____

Text: _____

Stopping point   **Reason for stopping**

1. _____   _____

                                         _____

2. _____   _____

                                         _____

3. _____   _____

                                         _____

4. _____   _____

                                         _____

5. _____   _____

                                         _____

6. _____   _____

                                         _____

7. _____   _____

                                         _____

Activities for Predicting/Guessing

The following two pages are reproducible activity sheets. These activity sheets are also available on the CD in the file titled, "EightB5."

S.O.L.V.E.

This activity makes a game of systematically working through the steps involved in coming up with a good inference. The activity may be completed as either a listening activity or a reading activity. The teacher should select a short text that contains plenty of action or suspense. Determine in advance of the lesson where the text should be segmented (three or four text chunks would be best). After reading (or hearing) each chunk, the readers/listeners respond to the questions set forth on the activity sheet, regarding clues in the text, personal connections, and compatibility with other clues. Then they make a prediction about what is likely to happen next. Readers/listeners complete this sequence of thinking after each subsequent text segment. This activity helps children learn how to keep their thinking on-track since it encourages them to revise their predictions as the author provides new evidence. Fun for all!

I Predict that I'll Remember. . .

This activity merges the strategy of Determining Important Clues with the idea of prediction. Students are asked to think about what they have learned from a text and what is important enough to them to remember for a very long time.

S.O.L.V.E.

Name: _____   Date: _____

Text: _____

S.O.L.V.E. is a good strategy for you to use when you are trying to predict what will happen next. After each chunk of text you:

Stop and think, and do the following:

Observe all of the important clues in the text, and write them in the first box.

Look for some connection to your own experiences, and write them in the second box.

Verify that all of the clues fit together, and put a "+" in the third box if all the clues fit.

Enter your best guess in the last box.

First stop

Text clues	My connections	+ or -	My best guess

Second stop

Text clues	My connections	+ or -	My best guess

Third stop

Text clues	My connections	+ or -	My best guess

I Predict that I'll Remember. . .

Name: _____   Date: _____

Text: _____

Here's what I learned: _____

_____.

Here's why I'll probably remember this information for a long time: _____

_____

_____.

Here's what I learned: _____

_____.

Here's why I'll probably remember this information for a long time: _____

_____

_____.

Here's what I learned: _____

_____.

Here's why I'll probably remember this information for a long time: _____

_____

_____.

Activities for Figuring Out
(Inferring)

The following two pages contain reproducible activity sheets. These activity sheets are also available on the CD in the file titled, "EightB6."

Character Study

Research consistently shows that students who understand the characters (or people) in a text generally demonstrate good comprehension of the main idea or theme of what they've read. But character traits are typically inferred, rather than stated directly. This activity is an acrostic that encourages students to reflect on a character's behavior or traits to understand that character more thoroughly.

A Message from the Author

This activity invites students to infer the theme or main idea of a text. Students identify the theme and then draw a parallel between the theme and the solution to or outcome of the problem. Finally, readers support their response with exact evidence from the text.

CHARACTER STUDY

Name: _____   Date: _____

Text: _____

Character's name: _____

Happiest when: _____

Acted like: _____

Responsible for: _____

Afraid of: _____

Concerned about: _____

Tried to: _____

Extremely: _____

Realized in the end that: _____

_____

A MESSAGE FROM THE AUTHOR

Name: _____   Date: _____

Text: _____

_____

In this text, I think the author wanted me to understand that _____

_____

_____

_____

I think this is the message because here's how the problem in this text got solved:

_____

_____

_____

_____

Here's a quote from the text that proves that this is the message: _____

_____

_____

_____

_____

Activities for Figuring Out
(Synthesizing)

The following four pages contain reproducible activity sheets. These activity sheets are also available on the CD in the file titled, "EightB6."

Summary Frame for Story Text

This simple-to-use graphic organizer provides a framework for students to recall the important parts of narrative text. The teacher's goal should be to gradually wean students from use of this organizer; the goal is for them to be able to construct a good summary independently.

Summary Frame for Informational Text

This organizer is similar to the one described above, but helps students to summarize informational text. Note that this format is ideal for expository materials that are organized around topics, main ideas, and details.

Important Words

This activity requires synthesis beyond just recall. Students need to identify several words important to the text and synthesize them into a cogent summary. (The teacher can determine beforehand how many vocabulary words students will need to incorporate.)

Three Points of View

This activity helps students recognize different voices on a particular topic — and find their own voice, as well. Students choose two texts that are paired for a particular purpose (similar theme, subject, problem, etc.). They write down a detail from the text that represents the thinking of the first author. Then they write down a detail from the text related to the point of view of the second author. Finally, they share their own point of view, making clear how the first two voices influenced (or failed to influence) their point of view.

SUMMARY FRAME FOR STORY TEXT

Name: _____   Date: _____

Text: _____

This story takes place _____.

The most important character is _____.

Other characters are _____

_____.

The problem that gets this story going is _____

_____.

When the characters try to solve this problem, here's what happens:

First, _____.

Second, _____.

Third, _____.

The problem is finally solved when _____

_____.

At the end of the story _____

_____.

From reading this story, I think the author wanted me to understand that _____

_____.

SUMMARY FRAME FOR INFORMATIONAL TEXT

Name: _____   Date: _____

Text: _____

The **topic** of this reading selection is _____.

The **main idea** is that _____
_____.

One **detail** that is important is _____
_____.

A second **detail** that is important is _____
_____.

A third **detail** that is important is _____
_____.

I think the author wrote about this topic because _____
_____
_____.

IMPORTANT WORDS

Name: _____   Date: _____

Text: _____

Choose _____ **important** words from the text. Write the words here:

_____   _____   _____

_____   _____   _____

_____   _____   _____

Now write a brief summary of this text using all of these important words.
Remember what needs to be included in a summary for a story and what needs to be
included in a summary for informational text.

_____

_____

_____

_____

_____

_____

_____

_____

_____

© 2004 Nancy N. Boyles, *Constructing Meaning*

THREE POINTS OF VIEW

Name: _____   Date: _____

Text # 1: _____

Author: _____

Point of view: _____

_____

_____

_____

Text # 2: _____

Author: _____

Point of view: _____

_____

_____

My point of view: _____

_____

_____

_____

Activities for Applying Strategies to Nonfiction

The following five pages are reproducible activity sheets. These activity sheets are also available on the CD in the file titled, "EightC."

Info-Gram and Info-Gram Lists

These organizers are designed to help students identify key points in informational texts and record them in a way that is easy to reference. One of these pages is specific to lists. The other page is a template that could be used for recording any category of information: people's names, places, dates, events, inventions, discoveries, other.

Good Questions to Ask

This form is useful for students to record questions to which they expect to find answers in a selection of informational text. Designating possible question stems that begin with who, what, where, when, why, and how is a helpful way for students to become alert to the kinds of questions that will probably be answered in the reading.

Question Cue-Cards

Each student should have his/her own set of Question Cue-Cards. I give each student a laminated set in a small envelope. Writing the student's name or initials on the back of the cards helps lost cards find their owners if they become misplaced. During small-group or large-group instruction, these cards are useful for monitoring strategy use. Students hold up their "Who" card, for example, if they locate an answer to a "who" question as we read through the text together.

I'm a Word Watcher

This form is a good place for students to collect words as they read informational text. Teachers (or students) can decide what kind of words will be included: unfamiliar words, bold-print words, names of people, words that seem important, etc. (Use the Mirror, Mirror. . . . activity as a second step in building vocabulary through informational text.)

INFO-GRAM:
(Important people, places, dates, events, inventions, discoveries, etc.)

Name: _____   Date: _____

Text: _____

Important _____   **Important because. . . . .**

_____   _____

_____   _____

_____   _____

_____   _____

_____   _____

_____   _____

_____   _____

_____   _____

_____   _____

_____

INFO-GRAM:
LISTS

Name: _____   Date: _____

Text: _____

List:

_____

_____

_____

_____

_____

_____

_____

_____

_____

_____

The author included this list because . . . .

_____

_____

_____

_____

_____

GOOD QUESTIONS TO ASK

Name: _____   Date: _____

Text: _____

Who: _____

_____

What: _____

_____

When: _____

_____

Where: _____

_____

Why: _____

_____

How: _____

_____

Who	**Where**
What	**Why**
When	**How**

I'M A WORD WATCHER

Name: _____   Date: _____

Text: _____

1. _____   11. _____

2. _____   12. _____

3. _____   13. _____

4. _____   14. _____

5. _____   15. _____

6. _____   16. _____

7. _____   17. _____

8. _____   18. _____

9. _____   19. _____

10. _____   20. _____

ANNOTATED BIBLIOGRAPHY
OF CHILDREN'S LITERATURE

Picture Books Perfect for Modeling Strategies

* Nonfiction or informational base
\# Expository format
(P) Great for primary

Texts to Encourage Students to Make *Connections*

Books useful for text-to-self connections contain common themes universal to childhood, such as friendship, sibling relationships, school issues, fear, jealousy, feeling different and other matters related to growing up. Lots of these texts are memoirs. And classic tales with a modern twist offer great possibilities for text-to-text connections.

*　　*Africa Brothers and Sisters* by Virginia Krol, New York: Aladdin Paperbacks, 1993.
　　　　A little boy finds similarities between himself and his "brothers and sisters" of numerous African tribes. Helps children find connections to others.

　　　Alaska's Three Pigs by Arlene Laverde, Seattle: Sasquatch Books, 2000.
　　　　Lots of text-to-text connections between this story and the classic version of the *Three Little Pigs*. Also introduces children to facts about Alaska's wildlife.

(P)　*Alexander and the Terrible, Horrible, No Good, Very Bad Day* by Judith Viorst, New York: Simon and Schuster, 1972.
　　　　Kids readily relate to the idea of a "very bad day" (teachers too!).

　　　All the Places to Love by Patricia MacLachlan, New York: Scholastic, 1994.
　　　　This memoir encourages children to think about the special places they love.

　　　All Those Secrets of the World by Jane Yolen, New York: Little, Brown, and Company, 1991.
　　　　It's hard to say good-bye.

　　　Angel Child, Dragon Child by Michele Surat, New York: Raintree Publishers, 1983.
　　　　A Vietnamese girl leaves her mother behind when she moves to America and faces many challenges in her new home.

(P)　*Annabelle Swift, Kindergartner* by Amy Schwartz, New York: Orchard Books, 1988.
　　　　Annabelle's sister helps prepare Annabelle for the first day of school, but she goes a bit overboard.

Appalachia: The Voices of Sleeping Birds by Cynthia Rylant, New York: Harcourt Brace and Company, 1991.
This story brings to life the similarities (and differences) between a wide range of communities.

(P) *Arthur's Teacher Trouble* by Marc Brown, New York: Little, Brown and Company, 1986.
Arthur has the strictest teacher in the school. Kids can relate!

Aunt Chip and the Great Triple Creek Dam Affair by Patricia Polacco, New York: Philomel Books, 1996.
Too much TV has negative consequences.

Book by George Ella Lyon, New York: DK Publishing, 1999.
Books open the door to a world of adventure.

(P) *A Chair for My Mother* by Vera Williams, New York: Greenwillow Books, 1982.
A family works together to save for something special after a fire destroys their home. Shows the love and mutual respect of an extended family.

(P) *Chrysanthemum* by Kevin Henkes, New York: Green Willow Books, 1991.
Children who do not like their name will relate to Chrysanthemum's plight. But in the end, she discovers her name is just right.

Dance on a Sealskin by Barbara Winslow, Anchorage (AK): Alaska Northwest Books, 1995.
This delightful tale about Yup'ik Eskimo culture depicts the thrill and anxiety of a coming-of-age ritual for a little girl. Captures the joy of giving and sharing among several generations.

(P) *Dandelion* by Don Freeman, New York: Puffin Books, 1977.
This very simple story reminds children of the consequences of vanity.

(P) *George and Martha* by James Marshall, Boston: Houghton Mifflin, 1972.
Five short stories perfect for primary level readers. Two lovable hippos encounter a host of people problems. Children will relate.

Gettin' through Thursday by Melrose Cooper, New York: Lee and Low Books, 1998.
Limited money leads to some sacrifices. But the book highlights the positive results that can come from families making sacrifices.

(P) *Hairs (Pelitos)* by Sandra Cisneros, New York: Alfred A. Knopf, 1994.
What sort of hair do you have? Is your hair like the hair of other people in your family? This very simple story will help young readers consider traits that they have in common and what makes them different from others.

*Home* by Thomas Locker, New York: Harcourt Books, 2000.
Poems that reflect on the corner of the world we each call home.

In My Family / En mi Familia by Carmen Garza, San Francisco: Children's Book Press, 1996.
This family album portraying everyday events as well as special moments in the life of an Hispanic family is narrated in both English and Spanish. The text could prompt children to celebrate their own cultural and family traditions in a similar memoir of their own.

In My Momma's Kitchen by Jerdine Nolen, New York: Scholastic, 1999.
Momma's kitchen was the setting for some very special memories. This memoir shows readers (and writers) the power of place in their lives.

(P) *Ira Sleeps Over* by Bernard Waber, Boston: Houghton Mifflin, 2000.
Should Ira admit to his friend that he just can't go to sleep without his favorite teddy bear? Little kids will really relate to Ira's plight (which has a happy ending!)

Just Us Women by Jeanette Caines, New York: Scholastic, 1982.
This memoir of a little girl taking a road trip with her favorite aunt will help students connect to the simple experiences in their own lives that are so special.

Keepers by Jeri Hanel Watts, New York: Lee and Low Books, 1997.
There are many issues here: a little boy who spends his money on a present for himself rather than a gift for his beloved grandmother, intergenerational love between a grandparent and a grandson, and the importance of keeping memories. Could be used with *The Giver*, by Lois Lowry.

(P) *Little Polar Bear* by Hans de Beer, New York: North-South Books, 1987.
Little Polar Bear gets lost and then finds his way back home, making some self-discoveries along the way.

Love You Forever by Robert Munsch, Willowdale (Ontario): Firefly Books, 1990.
Enduring nature of parents' love across generations.

 # * *Market* by Ted Lewin, New York: Harper Collins, 1996.
An international spin on "going to the mall."

More Than Anything Else by Marie Bradby, New York: Orchard Books, 1995.
Young Booker wants to read more than anything else. What can reading do for you? What do you want "more than anything else?"

(P) *My Dog is Lost* by Ezra Jack Keats and Pat Cherr, New York: Puffin Books, 1960.
A charming tale of a little boy in a new country who has lost his dog. His limited English makes the search more difficult. The story has plenty of connections for native Spanish speakers.

My Great Aunt Arizona by Gloria Houston, New York: Harper Collins, 1992.
It's all about teachers who make a difference, and the value of reading.

My Rotten Redheaded Older Brother by Patricia Polacco, New York: Simon and Schuster, 1994.
Competition between siblings, wanting to do something, *anything*, better than your older brother (sister).

The Pain and the Great One by Judy Blume, New York: Bradbury Press, 1985.
Sibling relationships, from both points of view—the older sister and the younger brother.

The Piano Man by Debbi Chocolate, New York: Walker and Company, 1998.
Her grandfather's passion for playing the piano created many family memories for this little girl. Ask your students, "What passions contribute to your life stories?"

Pigsty by Mark Teague, New York: Scholastic, 1994.
Lots of children will relate to this story of a very messy bedroom.

The Princess and the Pizza by Mary Jane and Herm Auch, New York: Scholastic: 2002
In this fractured fairytale, you will find a lot of humor that older students can appreciate. And there are plenty of opportunities to connect with other fairytales.

(P) *The Relatives Came* by Cynthia Rylant, New York: Simon and Schuster, 1985.
Visiting with relatives.

*Snapshots from the Wedding* by Gary Soto, New York: G.P. Putnam's Sons, 1997.
What's <u>really</u> in that picture? Good example of the power of small details.

Something Beautiful by Sharon Dennis Wyeth, New York: Bantam Doubleday Dell, 1998.
We can find beauty in our world regardless of our circumstances. This book will encourage students to *visualize*.

(P) *Stand Tall, Molly Lou Melon* by Patty Lovell, New York: Scholastic, 2001.
A good read-aloud for young children for positive self-image, facing adversity, and dealing with the class bully.

The Summer My Father was Ten by Pat Brisson, Honesdale (PA): Boyds Mills Press, 1998.
Intergenerational friendship grows out of a thoughtless childhood deed.

Tea with Milk by Allen Say, New York: Houghton Mifflin, 1999.
This book is about feeling like you don't fit in due to cultural differences.

Tell Me a Story, Mama by Angela Johnson, New York: Scholastic, 1989.
This memoir, written as a dialogue between a mother and her young daughter, shows the importance of the personal stories in our lives.

Thank You Mr. Falker by Patricia Polacco, New York: Philomel Books, 1998.
Learning difficulties, teasing, the importance of having a good and caring teacher.

Thomas' Snowsuit by Robert Munsch, Willowdale (Ontario): Firefly Books, 1997.
Power struggles between adults and children.

(P) *Twinnies* by Eve Bunting, New York: Harcourt, 1997.
Big brothers and sisters will relate to this tale of baby sibling(s) who seem to get ALL the attention. In the end, love prevails.

(P) *Umbrella* by Taro Yashima, New York: Puffin Books, 1986.
All young readers will relate to this story of a little Asian girl who has something brand new (an umbrella) and can hardly wait to use it.

(P) *Wemberly Worried* by Kevin Henkes, New York: Scholastic, 2000.
Wemberly is a little mouse who worries about everything and is especially worried about going to school. The worriers in your class will connect!

The Whale's Song by Dyan Sheldon, New York: Puffin Pied Piper Books, 1990.
The power of nature in one person's life.

(P) *What are YOU so grumpy about?* by Tom Lichtenheld, New York: Little, Brown and Company, 2003.
Great illustrations accompany this very up-beat grumpy book. Turns grumps into giggles.

What You Know First by Patricia MacLachlan, New York: Harper Collins, 1995.
It's hard to move to someplace new.

(P) *Whistle for Willie* by Ezra Jack Keats, New York: Puffin Books, 1964.
Willie wants to learn to whistle so he can call his dog. This story shows how perseverance and effort yield positive results.

The Wolf who Cried Boy by Bob Hartman, New York: G.P. Putnam's Sons, 2002.
This twisted tale offers many possibilities for text-to-text connections. Ask your students how it compares to the classic *The Boy who Cried Wolf*?

Books that lead students to think about injustices, tragedy and discrimination inspire them to wonder, "Why?"

Texts to Encourage Students to *Wonder*

Books that lead students to think about injustices, tragedy, discrimination, and other "heavy" themes ultimately inspire them to wonder "why." Questions will occur throughout the text, and many of those questions will remain unanswered at the end, resulting in your students' continued contemplation of the text and possibly even further inquiry.

*   *Aunt Harriet's Underground Railroad in the Sky* by Faith Ringgold, New York: Crown Publishers, 1992.
How does it feel to help slaves to escape to freedom?

Baseball Saved Us by Ken Mochizuki, New York: Lee and Low Books, 1993.
Focuses on life in a Japanese internment camp in post-WWII era. Leads to questions about treatment of the Japanese-Americans at this time in American history.

(P) *The Bracelet* by Yoshiko Uchida, New York: Philomel Books, 1993.
The subject here is also Japanese Internment camps and raises the same questions as above. A good book to help children make *connections*, too, especially in regards to friendships.

The Bus Ride by William Miller, New York: Lee and Low, 1998.
In this fictionalized version of the Rosa Parks story, a young girl stands up for what she believes. The story raises questions about Jim Crow laws of the past.

(P) *Dear Mr. Blueberry* by Simon James, New York: Simon and Schuster, 1996.
Deals with the issue of "what's real." Might also be appropriate for helping children to *notice* important details.

Dance on a Sealskin by Barbara Winslow, Anchorage (AK): Northwest Books, 1995.
This story describes a coming-of-age ceremony for a Yup'ik Eskimo girl in Alaska. You will want to ask your students, "What cultural traditions, customs, and rites-of-passage are important in your family?" And encourage them to ponder answers to this question.

*   *Faithful Elephants* by Yukio Tsuchiya, Boston: Houghton Mifflin, 1988.
Issues related to the devastating effects of war on <u>all</u> living creatures. For older readers.

The Flag We Love by Pam Munoz Ryan, Watertown (MA): Charlesbridge Publishing, 1996.
This text, told in rhyming verse, can inspire readers to consider the ideals that the American flag symbolizes for them. Great illustrations with a subtext that offers more elaboration.

*   *Goin' Someplace Special* by Patricia McKissack, New York: Scholastic, 2001.
Where is this "someplace special" and how did our country allow Jim Crow laws to dominate the lives of African Americans in the Southern states? This fictionalized account, based on the author's childhood, will likely provoke intense discussion.

Hey, Little Ant by Phillip and Hannah Hoose, New York: Scholastic, 1998.
This story is a dialogue between a kid and an ant about whether the kid should step on the ant. The reader must make the decision.

Katie's Trunk by Ann Turner, New York: Aladdin Paperbacks, 1992.
This story about the beginning of the American Revolution is told from the point of view of a young girl whose family sympathizes with the British. Will your students identify with this young girl?

Knots on a Counting Rope by Bill Martin Jr. and John Archambault, New York: Henry Holt and Company, 1987.
In this tale of intergenerational love and respect, a grandfather helps his grandson face his greatest challenge: blindness. The story helps children ponder their own special challenges and how they can face them.

* *Letting Swift River Go* by Jane Yolen, New York: Little, Brown and Company, 1992.
The towns along the Swift River in Massachusetts were drowned so that a reservoir could be created (Quabbin Reservoir) to supply water to the city of Boston. The story questions the value of the kind of "progress" that requires damning a wild river.

Miss Rumphius by Barbara Cooney, New York: Puffin Books, 1982.
Alice Rumphius is an old lady who has lived a long and productive life. She's traveled and had a lot of fun along the way. But she never forgot the wise words of her grandfather: "Do something to make the world more beautiful." Her example might encourage your students to consider their own worldly legacy.

Nim and the War Effort by Milly Lee, New York: Farrar Straus Giroux, 1997.
Set in San Francisco's Chinatown in 1943, Nim, a young Chinese-American girl, struggles to maintain loyalty to both her family and the American war effort. Be sure to ask your students, "Did Nim make the right decision?" The text lets the reader decide.

(P) * *Nobody Owns the Sky* by Reeve Lindbergh, Cambridge (MA): Candlewick Press, 1997.
This simple, poetic text about Bessie Coleman, the first licensed African American aviator, may leave children with a lot of questions about why race was such a factor in this woman's pursuit of a life-long dream.

One Yellow Daffodil: A Hanukkah Story by David Adler, New York: Harcourt Brace and Company, 1999.
Reliving past Hanukkah experiences helps Morris Kaplan come to terms with injustices done to him and his family in Poland during World War II. Why and how could these atrocities have occurred?

\# * *Peace Begins with You* by Katherine Scholes, New York: Little, Brown and Company, 1989.
The book helps children consider questions about peace. How do we protect peace? What are the consequences of not having peace?

(P) *Peppe the Lamplighter* by Elisa Bartone, New York: Lothrop, Lee & Shepard Books, 1993.
Peppe's family is very poor, so even though he is a small boy, he wants to have a job to earn some money. Unfortunately, his father thinks Peppe's job as a lamplighter is "beneath" him, and this judgment hurts Peppe a lot. What is a "good" job, anyway?

Pink and Say by Patricia Polacco, New York: Scholastic, 1994.
The book addresses treatment of African Americans in the South during the Civil War. Also a good book for *connections* regarding friendship.

*   *Richard Wright and the Library Card* by William Miller, New York: Scholastic, 1997.
> Issues surrounding the treatment of African Americans in the pre-Civil Rights South.

*   *The Royal Bee* by Frances Park and Ginger Park, Honesdale (PA): Boyds Mills Press, 2000.
> A poor Korean boy finds a way to receive an education and goes on to win a national award for his courage and intelligence. Encourages children to consider what having an education means to them and promotes other thoughtful questions, as well.

Running the Road to ABC by Denize Lauture, New York: Aladdin Paperbacks, 2000.
> Poetic text captures the exuberance of Haitian children on their way to school. Begs the question: What are you willing to sacrifice for your love of learning?

*   *Sadako* by Eleanor Coerr, New York: G. P. Putnam's Sons, 1993.
> This picture book version of this moving story will encourage many questions about the devastating effects of war. Although in many ways this is a tale of hope, the message ultimately comes to life through Sadako's death. May be too powerful for some children.

Sami and the Time of the Troubles by Florence Heide & Judith Gilliland, New York: Houghton Mifflin, 1992.
> Issues related to the devastating effects of war on both physical existence and the human spirit.

Scarecrow by Cynthia Rylant, New York: Harcourt, Inc., 2001.
> This beautifully written book begs the question: What makes life worth living? *That* question will generate plenty of thoughtful discussion!

*   *Star of Fear, Star of Hope* by Jo Hoestlandt, New York: Walker & Company, 1995.
> One day during World War II, Helen's best friend, Lydia, disappears never to be seen again. Where did Lydia go? A good starting point for a discussion about the Holocaust. Could be connected with *The Yellow Star* or *Number the Stars*.

(P)   *A Story for Bear* by Dennis Haseley, New York: Harcourt, Inc., 2002.
> What is the value of reading in your life? This beautifully illustrated book helps readers to consider that question. Lots of opportunities for personal connections here, too.

*   *The Story of Ruby Bridges* by Robert Coles, New York: Scholastic, 1995.
> Issues related to the desegregation of Southern schools in the 1960's.

Sweet Clara and the Freedom Quilt by Deborah Hopkinson, New York: Alfred A. Knopf, Inc., 1993.
> More questions about the Underground Railroad.

Tar Beach by Faith Ringgold, New York: Scholastic, 1991.
> Helps children consider the meaning of freedom.

The Three Questions (based on a story by Leo Tolstoy) by Jon Muth, New York: Scholastic, 2002.
> In this text, three important questions are asked: When is the best time to do things? Who is most important? What is the right thing to do? This is a beautifully illustrated story with an even more beautiful message.

*   *The Tree that Would Not Die* by Ellen Levine, New York: Scholastic, 1995.
This story, which is rooted in fact, is told from the tree's point of view and raises questions about misuse of the natural environment.

Weslandia by Paul Fleischman, Cambridge (MA): Candlewick Press, 1999.
Wesley, the school outcast, decides that a fun summer project will be the creation of his own civilization. Beyond issues of Wesley's socialization, students will have a lot to think about as they question just how a civilization is established. For older readers.

Whitewash by Ntozake Shange, New York: Walker and Company, 1997.
Issues related to racially motivated hate crimes.

*   *The Wild Boy* by Mordicai Gerstein, New York: Farrar Straus Giroux, 1998.
This book for older readers is based on the true story of "Victor," a wild boy discovered in the forests of southern France in 1800. Readers will have many questions about Victor's treatment in "civilization" as they speculate about his past and ponder ethical issues.

(P)   *Wilfrid Gordon McDonald Partridge* by Mem Fox, New York: Kane/Miler, 1985.
Addresses the topic of memories and what they're made of. Good for connections, too.

Wings by Christopher Myers, New York: Scholastic, 2000.
Main character is Ikarus Jackson, who uses his beautiful wings to fly— despite the scorn he faces from peers for being so different. Lends itself to questions about embracing differences and celebrating individuality.

Books with vivid language help readers to create mental images and other sensory impressions.

Texts to Encourage Use of the *Picturing* Strategy
(Using the five senses to understand text)

Books with vivid language that create sensory impressions, including images in the reader's mind offer rich possibilities. Such books may not be the best "stories." They show, rather than tell, and allow readers to draw their own conclusions in response to a mental picture and other sensory impressions.

Africa Dream by Eloise Greenfield, New York: Harper Collins, 1977.
A child is transported in a dream back to the long-ago Africa of her ancestors.

America the Beautiful, Poem by Katherine Lee Bates illustrated by Neil Waldman, New York: Aladdin Paperbacks, 1993.
Gorgeous acrylic paintings accompany the words to this patriotic poem. What do students visualize as *they* hear the words of this time-honored classic?

The Bunyans by Audrey Wood, New York: Scholastic, 1996.
This larger-than-life tall tale creates some wild visual images in the reader's mind, providing outlandish explanations of several U.S. geographical features.

(P)   *The Cow who Wouldn't Come Down* by Paul Brett Johnson, New York: Scholastic, 1993.
This silly story about a flying cow invites the reader (or listener) to create comical visual images to accompany the fanciful text.

*   *The Desert is Theirs* by Byrd Baylor, New York: Aladdin Paperbacks, 1975.
Integrates myth, folklore and factual description into a kaleidoscope of images of desert life.

Every Time I Climb a Tree by David McCord, New York: Little, Brown and Company, 1980.
Twenty five charming poems for young children create whimsical images.

The Fungus that Ate My School by Arthur Dorros, New York: Scholastic, 2000.
Kids will have a great time imagining this classroom scene, a school-eating fungus.

(P)   *How Do Dinosaurs Say Good Night?* by Jane Yolen, New York: Scholastic, 2000.
Can *you* picture what happens when Mom and Dad try to put the family dinosaur to bed? Young children will love the big, bold illustrations by Mark Teague.

I am the Mummy Heb-Nefert by Eve Bunting, New York: Harcourt, Inc., 1997.
Heb-Nefert, once a wealthy Egyptian woman, is now a mummy encased in glass in a museum. She recalls her life of luxury in such stunning detail that your students will vividly picture her former lavish life.

*   *I Have Heard of a Land* by Joyce Carol Thomas, New York: Harper Collins Publishers, 1998.
Powerful images of the strength and courage of people who headed to the Oklahoma Territory in the 1880s to obtain free land. Especially focuses on strong women.

I Say a Little Prayer for You adapted from the original song by Burt Bacharach and Hal David, New York: Scholastic, 2002.
The lyrics to this song are accompanied by lively illustrations that represent one person's interpretation of these words. Good model for students to use for a similar activity.

I Stink by Kate and Jim McMullan, New York: Harper Collins Publishers, 2002.
Who'd ever think that a book about a garbage truck would be a great teaching tool! This story is told from the truck's point of view. It's a feast for all of the senses. You can point out the way the text *looks*, too. (Kids can try this approach in their own writing.)

In November by Cynthia Rylant, New York: Harcourt, Inc., 2000.
Rylant's usual word-artistry leaves plenty of room for readers to create their own multi-sensory images around the magic of November.

Is that You, Winter? by Stephen Gammell, New York: Harcourt, Inc., 1997.
This simple text can be appreciated at a variety of levels. Winter is personified in this story. How do you visualize "old man winter"?

Lift Ev'ry Voice and Sing by James Weldon Johnson, New York: Scholastic, 1995.
The lyrics to this song are illustrated with amazing paintings. Might inspire students to illustrate a song or poem they love.

(P)   *Little White Dog* by Laura Godwin, New York: Hyperion Books, 1998.
A playful, simple text for younger readers. Challenges them to find a little white dog and his many friends by discerning figure/ground relationships.

(P)   *More Parts* by Tedd Arnold, New York: Scholastic, 2001.
Cleverly told story based on literal translations of figurative expressions (e.g., "Give me a hand.")

My Mama Had a Dancing Heart by Libba Moore Gray, New York: Grolier, 1995.
> The words almost "dance off the page" here in this journey through the seasons. Also good for *connecting* to mother/child relationships.

Night in the Country by Cynthia Rylant, New York: Aladdin Paperbacks, 1991.
> A vision of nighttime—with Rylant's magical touch.

(P) *No Jumping on the Bed!* by Ted Arnold, New York: Penguin Books, 1987.
> When this little boy jumps on his bed, he crashes through the floor and into the lives of other families in his apartment building. Let your students picture these situations mentally before you show them the illustrations.

Owl Moon by Jane Yolen, New York: Philomel Books, 1987.
> Depicts the special companionship of a young child and her father, as well as a multi-sensory exploration of the natural world. Exquisite illustrations!

Reflections by Ann Jonas, New York: Greenwillow Books, 1987.
> Read from the first to the last page, then turn the book upside down to complete the story and make an amazing visual discovery!

Round Trip by Ann Jonas, New York: Greenwillow Books, 1983.
> Same concept as above, different topic, this time in black and white.

The School Nurse from the Black Lagoon by Mike Thaler, New York: Scholastic, 1995.
> Great visual images with a funny twist. (See other *Black Lagoon* books for more humorous school-related images.)

The Seashore Book by Charlotte Zolotow, New York: Harper Collins, 1992.
> All of the senses come to life in this trip to the beach in summer. You and your students will find a lot of similes to *notice* in regards to author's craft.

(P) *Snow Bear* by Jean Craighead George, New York: Hyperion Books, 1999.
> This very simple story is set against a dramatic arctic backdrop of towering glaciers and frozen ice ships, inspiring many sensory impressions for attentive readers.

Swamp Angel by Ann Isaacs, New York: Puffin Books, 1994.
> A typical tall tale with some pretty sophisticated humor encourages fun visual images and is also good for *noticing* elements of humor.

Tomas and the Library Lady, by Pat Mora, New York: Dragonfly Books, 2000.
> This story of a little boy who thrives on library books describes how he visualizes the scenes in the stories he reads. Tomas models the think-aloud process as he describes the pictures he makes in his mind!

Through Grandpa's Eyes by Patricia MacLachlan, Harper Collins, 1980.
> John spends the day with his blind grandfather and "sees" the world through his eyes. The book addresses the concept of visualizing.

Tulip Sees America by Cynthia Rylant, New York: Scholastic, 1998.
> This very simple text describes seeing the sights and sounds of the American landscape for the first time.

\# * *Welcome to the Greenhouse* by Jane Yolen, New York: Putnam and Grosset, 1993.
> A vivid and poetic tour of the rain forest.

\# * *Welcome to the Sea of Sand* by Jane Yolen, New York: Penguin Putnam Books, 1996.
> A vivid and poetic tour of the Sonora Desert.

When I Was Young in the Mountains by Cynthia Rylant, New York: Penguin Books, 1982.
    Demonstrates the power of simple nouns to create pictures in the reader's mind and shows that good description need not rely on adjectives.

Yankee Doodle by Steven Kellogg, New York: Aladdin Paperbacks, 1996.
    This song creates mental pictures for readers and listeners.

Zoom by Istvan Banyai, New York: Puffin Books, 1995.
    This wordless picture book gives the reader plenty to think about. Watch the ever-expanding image zoom from close-up to panoramic-plus! (If you like this book, check out *Re-Zoom* by the same author.)

Texts that Encourage *Figuring Out*
(Inferring)

Texts useful for modeling the inferring strategy typically offer readers a strong message that is implied, rather than stated directly. The author "shows," rather than "tells." The real meaning of these stories goes deeper than the events that unfold in the plot. The lesson or message of the story may not be clear immediately after reading, but begins to take shape with continued contemplation and reflection.

Abuela by Arthur Dorros, New York: Puffin Books, 1997.
    Students can infer the meaning of Spanish phrases sprinkled throughout this imaginative adventure. Helps children learn how to discern meaning from context.

* *Alejandro's Gift* by Richard Albert, San Francisco: Chronicle Books, 1994.
    This uplifting story about life in a desert has a strong message about the natural environment.

Aurora: A Tale of the Northern Lights by Mindy Dwyer, Cnachorage (AK): Alaska Northwest Books, 1997.
    This fanciful legend about an Alaskan girl and the origin of the Aurora Borealis leads readers to a message for their own lives. The book is great for *visualizing*, too.

A Bad Case of Stripes by David Shannon, New York: Scholastic, 1998.
    Camilla Cream is too concerned with the opinions of her friends and reluctant to stand up for what she wants. She ends up with a peculiar ailment that is cured, at last, only by her expression of her secret passion.

The Crane Wife by Odds Bodkin, New York: Harcourt, Inc., 1998.
    This Japanese folktale shows the unfortunate outcome of personal greed. The illustrations are incredible, and you and your students will find many opportunities for text-to-text connections from this story to others.

Fables by Arnold Lobel, New York: Harper and Row, 1980.
    These fables have a modern, funny twist. Students of all ages love them.

(P) *Frederick* by Leo Lionni, New York: Dragonfly Books, 1987.
    This fable about a little mouse who dreams rather than works makes it clear that sometimes dreams are as important as life's day-to-day drudgery.

The King's Equal by Katherine Paterson, New York: Harper Collins, 1992.
    This fairy tale in brief, chapter-book form offers opportunities for using *all* strategies as the king tries to find himself an "equal" to marry. In addition to considering the important lesson of the story, students can try to define wealth and predict the outcome of this royal dilemma.

(P) *Koala Lou* by Mem Fox, New York: Harcourt Brace & Company, 1989.
Kids can *figure out* from this animal tale that a parent's love is ever-present, not something that must be earned.

Leah's Pony by Elizabeth Friedrich, Honesdale, (PA): Boyds Mills Press, 1996.
This simple story of family love during Depression-era America provides many reminders about what really matters in life and raises some interesting questions about ethics.

The Legend of the Bluebonnet by Tomie dePaola, New York: Scholastic, 1983.
This Native American folktale tells of a little girl who gives up her most valued possession for the well being of her community. Even young children can infer the author's message, the value of selfless love.

(P) *The Lion who Wanted to Love* by Giles Andreae, London: Orchard Books, 1997.
This is a charming story for younger children, told entirely in rhyme, about love conquering all.

The Lotus Seed by Tatsuro Kiuchi, New York: Harcourt Brace & Company, 1993.
How does a simple lotus seed become a symbol of hope for members of a Vietnamese family separated from their homeland?

Miz Berlin Walks by Jane Yolen, New York: Puffin Books, 1997.
What is the power of a good story? Ask your students about stories that have special meaning in their life. This book is good for making *connections*, too.

Nappy Hair by Carolivia Herron, New York: Dragonfly Books, 1997.
This story is told in dialect using a call-and-response format. The sound of the language contributes to the clear message about the wonder of "nappy hair."

Night Golf by William Miller, New York: Lee and Low Books, 1999.
This is the true story of an African-American boy who confronts racial barriers on the golf course. Children can learn a lot from this little-known corner of American sports history.

Nobiah's Well: A Modern African Folktale by Donna Guthrie, New York: Scholastic: 1993.
The book offers a message your students will ponder: "When digging a well it must be as deep as your heart and as wide as your thirst."

Now One Foot, Now the Other by Tomie dePaola, New York: G. P. Putnam's Sons, 1981.
In this sensitive inter-generational story, children discover that a grandpa's love for his grandson is reciprocated when Grandpa has a stroke, and his grandson then teaches him.

(P) *Officer Buckle and Gloria* by Peggy Rathman, New York: G. P. Putnam's and Sons, 1995.
Officer Buckle thinks the children are listening attentively to his safety tips. But readers quickly figure out that the real star of the show is a dog named Gloria.

The Paper Bag Princess by Robert Munsch, New York: Firefly Books, 1980.
This fairy tale with a "strong girl" theme is enjoyed by readers of all ages and dispels the stereotypic "princess" image.

The Polar Express by Chris Van Allsburg, Boston: Houghton Mifflin, 1985.
This moving tale invokes the magic of a Christmas bell to consider the mystery of *what is real*.

Texts useful for modeling the inferring strategy offer readers a strong message that is implied.

Princess Penelope's Parrot by Helen Lester, Boston: Houghton Mifflin, 1996.
This funny story about the disastrous results of bad manners could be compared with *The Paper Bag Princess*. In this story, too, the *princess* is badly behaved. Many opportunities to use all comprehension strategies.

The Quilt Maker's Gift by Jeff Brumbeau, Daluth (MN): Pfeifer-Hamilton, Inc., 2000.
This modern-day fable celebrates the joy of giving. Quilt squares that symbolize different aspects of life add to the mystery of the story.

(P) *The Rainbow Fish* by Marcus Pfister, New York: North-South Books, 1992.
A fable about the joy of giving, but less abstract than the story above.

(P) *Regards to the Man in the Moon* by Ezra Jack Keats, New York: Aladdin Paperbacks, 1981.
Perfect for primary-age students, this tale about the power of the imagination addresses the issue of pride in one's work, regardless of social status.

The Rough-Face Girl by Rafe Martin, New York: Puffin Books, 1992.
In this Algonquin Cinderella, readers discover that a scarred face can't disguise the beauty and kindness of this girl's heart.

* *Salt in His Shoes: Michael Jordan in Pursuit of a Dream* by Deloris Jordan, New York: Simon and Schuster, 2000.
The mother of basketball superstar Michael Jordan shares her recollections of her son's pursuit of his dream in the face of adversity. The story offers a message of hope, faith, and family togetherness.

Sister Anne's Hands by Marybeth Lorbiecki, New York: Puffin Books, 1998.
Sister Anne's hands are brown, and Anna's hands are white. It's the early 1960s, and racial discrimination abounds in white, middle class schools. The story offers insight into the coming to terms with racial differences.

Slow Loris by Alexis Deacon, La Jolla (CA): Kane/Miller Publishers, 2002.
People (and things) are not always as they appear. So don't be too quick to jump to conclusions. Children will enjoy the creative graphics as they consider how the lesson learned from Slow Loris can make a difference in their own lives.

Some Frog by Eve Bunting, New York: Harcourt, Inc., 1998.
Billy learns some important lessons through his school's frog-jumping contest. He learns, not just about jumping frogs, but also about dads who make promises and don't keep them. The story offers a sensitive treatment of a difficult subject.

Squids Will Be Squids by John Scieszka, New York: Penguin Putnam Books, 1998.
Can you and your students figure out the morals to these up-beat, contemporary fables?

(P) *Tacky the Penguin* by Helen Lester, Boston: Houghton Mifflin, 1988.
Tacky was an "odd bird." But, in the end, his unwillingness to follow the pack saved the day. Even young readers will be able to infer from this story that unanticipated adventures can result from being true to your self.

* *Teammates* by Peter Golenbock, New York: Harcourt Brace & Company, 1990.
Many defining moments were in store for Jackie Robinson as well as Pee Wee Reese as the Brooklyn Dodgers brought the first-ever African-American player onto a major league baseball team. We can all learn something from this tale of courage and character.

Uncle Jed's Barbershop by Margaree King Mitchell, New York: Scholastic, 1993.
Uncle Jed's unique personal traits helped make his dream reality. Your students will *figure out* the key to his success.

* *The Yellow Star* by Carmen Agra Deedy, Atlanta: Peachtree Publishers, 2000.
How will King Christian X of Denmark preserve the unity of the Danes amid Nazi attempts to terrorize Jewish people?

Yo! Yes? By Chris Raschka, New York: Scholastic, 1993.
With only one or two words per page, readers have a lot to *figure out* from the expressive illustrations. And children can use this text as a springboard to help them think about how *they* form friendships.

You Are Special by Max Lucado, New York: Scholastic, 1997.
Little wooden people called Wemmicks get gold stars if they are pretty and talented or ugly gray dots if they are imperfect. With the help of Eli the woodcarver, Punchinello understands that he is special, regardless of what other Wemmicks think of him.

Texts to Encourage Use of the *Figuring Out* Strategy
(Synthesis)

Texts that encourage synthesis require readers to do more than collect details of the story for summarization. Synthesis is a matter of seeing how the details fit together to draw a conclusion, how the details solve a mystery, or how they bring characters (and readers) to a new understanding. Synthesis involves an "aha" moment, when, all of a sudden, everything becomes clear. Using more than one text, helping students to integrate information from two or more sources, is another way of helping them learn to *synthesize*, to *figure out*.

Araminta's Paint Box by Karen Ackerman, New York: Aladdin Paperbacks, 1990.
Araminta thinks her paint box is lost as her family heads west with the pioneers. But Araminta's paint box enjoys an adventure of its own. Readers can speculate how Araminta and her paint box may ultimately reconnect.

* *Beast Feast* by Douglas Florian, New York: Harcourt Brace & Company, 1994.
Short poems about different animals. Creative teachers will easily convert them to riddles which students may then solve.

(P) *The Bookstore Ghost* by Barbara Maitland, New York: Puffin Books, 1998.
This easy-to-read book offers up a mystery for young readers to *figure out*: who is the bookstore ghost?

(P) *The Cake that Mack Ate* by Rose Robart, New York: Little, Brown and Company, 1986.
A funny, cumulative tale with a surprise ending. Even when the reader *synthesizes* all of the information, Mack's identity remains a mystery.

Dear Mrs. LaRue: Letters from Obedience School by Mark Teague, New York: Scholastic, 2002.
This funny story, written in the voice of Ike, the dog, will get readers thinking about how Ike's bad habits may serve a useful purpose. Encourage your students to find the clues the author provides.

The Gardener by Sarah Stewart, New York: Farrar, Strais Gorpix, 1997.
What will make Lydia Grace's uncle smile? Use the author's clues to predict the story's outcome.

(P) *The Gingerbread Boy* by Richard Egielski, New York: Harper Collins, 1997.
An updated, urban version of the classic tale. Will the gingerbread boy outsmart the fox, or will the fox win this time, too? Sooner or later, children will *figure out* the outcome of this adventure.

(P) *Hooway for Wodney Wat* by Helen Lester, Boston: Houghton Mifflin, 1999.
Clever children will *figure out* the word play in this amusing text and predict the actions of this shy little rodent who cannot pronounce the letter, "*r*." The book offers many opportunities for using *all* strategies.

* *In the Swim* by Douglas Florian, New York: Harcourt, Inc., 1997.
Poems about things that swim. Prior knowledge will be a factor in enjoying these playful rhymes about various sea creatures.

(P) *It Begins with an A* by Stephanie Calmenson, New York: Scholastic, 1993.
An A-Z look at riddles provide a series of clues for young children to *synthesize*.

(P) *Martha Speaks* by Susan Meddaugh, Boston, Houghton Mifflin, 1992.
Martha, the family dog, learns to talk! At first her family thinks this is very cool, but Martha's words begin to create some embarrassing situations. How will this situation resolve itself? Readers can try to *figure out* the outcome for themselves.

The Mysteries of Harris Burdick by Chris Van Allsburg, Boston: Houghton Mifflin, 1984.
Integrate each bizarre black-and-white illustration with its accompanying title and single line of text to unravel a story. This book correlates well with writing activities.

* *On the Wing* by Douglas Florian, New York: Harcourt, Inc., 1996.
More poems, this time about birds. Some of these are pretty obscure, but others work well in a "riddle" format.

(P) *The Stray Dog* by Marc Simont, New York: Scholastic, 2001.
Good story for young children about how a stray dog comes to find a family of his own. Many opportunities for *predictions*.

Thirteen Moons on Turtle's Back by Joseph Bruchac and Jonathan London, New York: Philomel Books, 1992.
Ask your students to *figure out* the months of the Native American year based on text clues and illustrations.

The Toll-Bridge Troll by Patricia Rae Wolff, New York: Harcourt, 1995.
Trigg is confronted by a scary troll on his way to school each day. Trigg figures out a plan to ask riddles of the troll. The plan works, sort of. Kids will enjoy trying to outsmart the scary troll along with Trigg.

Under the Lemon Moon by Edith Hope Fine, New York: Lee and Low Books, 1999.
This multi-cultural tale explores themes of justice and compassion. Will children be able to *figure out* the solution to Rosalinda's problem?

Voices in the Park by Anthony Browne, New York: DK Publishing, Inc., 1998.
This simple story is written from four different points of view. Students will be intrigued *figuring out* how these various voices fit into one story.

\# *   *Water Dance* by Thomas Locker, New York: Harcourt Brace & Company, 1997.
Many fascinating facts about water are presented as riddles, complementing a poetic text and inspiring paintings.

(P)   *What Am I? An Animal Guessing Game* by Iza Trapani, New York: Scholastic: 1992.
Animal riddles with whimsical illustrations, just right for young children.

(P)   *A Wolf at the Door* by Nick Ward, New York: Scholastic, 2001.
Provides an opportunity for young children to use their text-to-text *connections* to *predict* the surprising outcome of this adventure.

The Wretched Stone by Chris Van Allsburg, Boston: Houghton Mifflin, 1991.
Clues throughout the text help the reader determine the identity of "the wretched stone." Excellent for kids who can think abstractly.

Texts to Encourage Use of the *Predicting/Guessing* Strategy

Students should make predictions as they read *any* text. The structure of a text, as well as its plot and illustrations, can inspire readers to guess or predict what will happen next. The following books encourage students to make a variety of predictions.

(P)   *If the World Ran out of B's* by Samantha and Bill Shireman, Hillsboro (OR): Beyond Words Publishing, 2002.
This clever text can be enjoyed by very young children (as it reinforces phonemic awareness) and also appreciated by older readers, who can recognize the word-play concept and apply it to some writing of their own.

(P)   *Animalogies* written and illustrated by fourth grade students of Six-to-Six Interdistrict Magnet School in Bridgeport, CT, New York: Scholastic, 2003.
This clever book by student authors introduces children to analogies in a way that is easy to understand and visually appealing.

(P)   *Guess whose Shadow?* by Stephen Swinburne, New York: Scholastic, 1999.
Wonderful photographs help young students *predict* whose shadow they are seeing—before they turn the page.

(P)   *Hog-Eye* by Susan Meddaugh, Boston: Houghton Mifflin, 1995.
A little pig outsmarts a hungry wolf. Will young readers be able to predict the little pig's next clever move?

(P)   *It Looked Like Spilt Milk* by Charles Shaw, New York: Harper Collins, 1947.
A very simple text invites readers to *figure out* exactly what it was that looked like spilt milk. Good for early primary grades.

Joseph Had a Little Overcoat by Simms Taback, New York: Scholastic, 1999.
Joseph turns his ragged overcoat into a jacket, then into smaller and smaller items of clothing. What will it become next?

Too Many Tamales by Gary Soto, New York: Scholastic, 1993.
Encourages students to predict how Mama will get her diamond ring back.

Every text contains important ideas, words, and details that help readers construct meaning.

Texts to Encourage *Noticing* Clues to Meaning

Every text contains important ideas, words, and details that help readers construct meaning. Don't overlook fiction in your quest for texts to help you teach children to *notice* important textual clues. However, nonfiction, informational text, in its many forms, offers abundant opportunities for teaching this strategy since the foremost mission of nonfiction is to convey factual content. Informational text comes in many forms; several are specified below.

Picture Book Biographies

These books, due to the brevity of the picture-book format, often depict only a segment of the individual's life, rather than a complete account.

* *Dinner at Aunt Connie's House*, by Faith Ringgold, New York: Scholastic, 1997.
This story-within-a-story provides brief biographies of 12 notable black women. Effective format.

* *Eleanor* by Barbara Cooney, New York: Scholastic, 1996.
Explores the less-than-happy childhood of American First Lady Eleanor Roosevelt, especially the role one special teacher played in helping Eleanor triumph over her fears.

* *George Washington: A Picture Book Biography* by James Giblin, New York: Scholastic, 1992.
Beautiful oil paintings accompany this simply told story of our first president.

(P) * *Honest Abe* by Edith Kunhardt and Malcah Zeldis, New York: Mulberry Books, 1993.
A simple text with incredible pictures. Children will find lots of important details of Abe's life.

* *Mandela* by Floyd Cooper, New York: Puffin Books, 1996.
A moving story of a contemporary civil rights leader who stood firm for what was fair and right for black people in South Africa.

* *Meet My Grandmother: She's a Supreme Court Justice* by Lisa Tucker McElroy (with help from Courtney O'Connor), Brookfield (CT): Millbrook Press, 1999.
Nice text and photos of Justice Sandra Day O'Connor–from a kid's point of view.

* *Minty: A Story of Young Harriet Tubman* by Alan Schroeder, New York: Puffin Books, 1996.
This touching story, with pictures as powerful as its words, focuses on Harriet as a child.

* *My Dream of Martin Luther King* by Faith Ringgold, New York: Crown Publishers, 1995.
Chronicles MLK's life and his role in the Civil Rights Movement.

* *Satchmo's Blues* by Alan Schroeder, New York: Random House, 1996.
There's a lot of kid appeal in this story of the childhood of Louis Armstrong.

* *Snowflake Bentley* by Jacqueline Briggs Martin, Boston: Houghton Mifflin, 1998.
Wilson Bentley, often misunderstood in his own time, perceived snowflakes as small miracles. His photography captured beautiful images of snowflakes. And his story demonstrates both a scientist's vision and a personal passion for nature. Caldecott Award

* *Starry Messenger* by Peter Sis, New York: Farrar Straus Giroux, 1996.
Celebrates the life and genius of Galileo by looking at the man, not just his accomplishments. Side bars and other incidental text add detail and depth.

* *Talkin' about Bessie: The Story of Aviator Elizabeth Coleman* by Nikki Grimes, New York: Scholastic, 2002.
This story of Bessie Coleman's life is told by different family members and friends who knew her. This story helps to teach narrative point of view.

Historical Fiction

You will find some of these texts, which feature fictitious characters in real situations, elsewhere in this bibliography, too

* *Nettie's Trip South* by Ann Turner, New York: Aladdin paperbacks, 1987.
Nettie describes her trip to the South before the Civil War, including her encounter with slaves and her impressions of a slave auction she attends.

* *A River Ran Wild* by Lynne Cherry, New York: Scholastic, 1992.
With powerful illustrations and text, this story describes the contrasting philosophies which Native Americans and European settlers in the New World held in regards to the natural environment.

* *Sarah Morton's Day* by Kate Waters, New York: Scholastic, 1989.
A fictionalized version of a day in the life of a Pilgrim girl in Plymouth, with wonderful photographs.

* *She's Wearing a Dead Bird on Her Head!* by Kathryn Lasky, New York: Hyperion Books, 1995.
Harriet Hemenway and Minna Hall crusade against the practice of wearing "dead birds" on ladies hats, and the Massachusetts Audubon Society is born. Great illustrations.

* *The Tree that Would Not Die* by Ellen Levine New York: Scholastic, 1995.
This tale of the Treaty Oak in Texas, and how the tree was nearly destroyed, is told from the tree's point of view.

Narrative/Poetic Nonfiction

These texts present factual information through a story format, making their content more accessible and meaningful for even young readers.

(P) * *Antarctica* by Helen Cowcher, New York: Farrar Straus Giroux, 1990.
Describes the winter life of penguins and seals and the spring invasion of a new presence that threatens their fragile world.

(P) * *Blast Off! Poems about Space* by Selected by Lee Bennett Hopkins, New York: Harper Collins, 1995.
This Level 3, *I Can Read Book* presents 20 simple poems that explain space concepts in easy-to-understand terms.

(P) *Bugs for Lunch* by Margery Facklam, Watertown (MA): Charlesbridge Publishing, 1999.
Rhymed verses and bright paintings introduce young listeners to a variety of creatures that eat insects. Good for primary science connections.

*   *Cactus Hotel* by Brenda Guiberson, New York: Henry Holt and Company, 1991.
       This story relies on a kid-friendly metaphor, a cactus hotel, to weave scientific facts into a simple tale of a fragile ecosystem.

*   *A Caribou Journey* by Debbie Miller, New York: Little, Brown and Company, 1994.
       Vividly portrays seasonal changes in the land and life cycle of the caribou. Great source of information and well-told story.

*   *A Drop Around the World* by Barbara Shaw McKinney, Nevada City (CA): DAWN Publications, 1998.
       Traveling with "Drop," readers see the world from different viewpoints, solid, liquid, and vaporous. The story is presented cleverly in rhyme.

*   *The Eyes of Gray Wolf* by Jonathan London, San Francisco: Chronicle Books, 1993.
       Readers follow gray wolf as he wanders through a winter night. The factual narrative is enhanced by spectacular illustrations.

*   *The Great Kapok Tree* by Lynn Cherry, New York, Harcourt, Inc., 1990.
       This fact-based story of the Amazon rain forest, replete with vivid illustrations, invites children to *notice* the many ways that human and animal life are harmed by deforestation.

*   *How to Dig a Hole to the Other Side of the World* by Faith McNulty, New York: Harper Collins, 1979.
       Great information about the center of the earth, conveyed in a narrative format. The content is accessible to even fairly young children.

One Tiny Turtle by Nicola Davies, New York: Scholastic, 2001.
       This easy to understand book about the life of the Loggerhead turtle is informative and visually appealing. (One of my favorite books)

*   *Over the Top of the World* by Will Steger, New York: Scholastic, 1997.
       Sharp photographs, interesting journal entries, and lots of information about Arctic travel are packed into this true account of Steger's 1995 expedition across the North Pole.

*   *Scruffy: A Wolf Finds his Place in the Pack* by Jim Brandenburg, New York: Walker and Company, 1996.
       Dramatic photos accompany this narrative about the lives of wolves, and, in particular, a wolf pup named, "Scruffy." Filled with factual details.

*   *Talking Walls* by Margy Burns Knight, Gardiner (ME): Tilbury House Publishers, 1992.
       In very readable style, this book explores famous walls around the world, showing the impact of walls on people who are divided or united by these partitions.

*   *To the Top of the World: Adventures with Arctic Wolves* by Jim Brandenburg, New York: Walker and Company, 1993.
       First-hand account of a wildlife photographer's experience following a wild wolf pack. Incredible photographs accompany the narrative, which is in the style of a journal. For older readers.

*   *The Whales* by Cynthia Rylant, New York: Scholastic, 1996.
       A lyrical prose poem brings to life these regal creatures, accompanied by vivid paintings.

Informational Books with an Expository Format

Some of these books contain features typically found in expository text (tables of contents, subheadings, etc.) Others do not have these features, but still present information as facts, rather than story.

\# *   *And So They Build* by Bert Kitchen, Cambridge (MA): Candlewick Press, 1993.
Why do different animals build their marvelous structures? This book explains why, with superb artwork that shows these structures, up close.

\# *   *The BOAT Alphabet Book* by Jerry Pallotta, Watertown (MA): Charlesbridge Publishing, 1998.
Features boats past and present, incorporating informative descriptions and dramatic illustrations.

\# *   *The Day Martin Luther King, Jr. Was Shot* by Jim Haskins, New York: Scholastic, 1992.
A photo history of the Civil Rights Movement. For older readers.

(P) \# *   *Hats, Hats, Hats* by Ann Morris, New York: Scholastic, 1989.
Bright, bold illustrations are matched to a simple listing of different kinds of hats. This book is a good model for early writing, in which students make lists of various items.

\# *   *The Heart* by Seymour Simon (or any book by Seymour Simon), New York: Scholastic, 1996.
This author explores scientific topics with readable text and up-close illustrations that bring the text to life.

\# *   *Immigrant Kids* by Russell Freedman, New York: Scholastic, 1980.
Depicts the daily life of children who came to this country through Ellis Island in the late 1800s and early 1900s. For older readers.

\# *   *Knights in Shining Armor* by Gail Gibbons (or any book by Gail Gibbons), New York: Little, Brown and Company, 1995.
This author has written and illustrated more than 80 informational books for children, turning fact into entertainment. Her other titles include *Click! A Book about Cameras and Taking Pictures.*

\# *   *Oh, Freedom* by Casey King and Linda Osborne, New York: Scholastic, 1997.
Kids talk about the Civil Rights Movement with the people who made it happen. Includes many interviews with famous and not-so-famous people.

(P) \# *   *Puffins Climb, Penguins Rhyme* by Bruce McMillan, New York: Harcourt, Inc., 1995.
This is a very simple book, but would be great to help primary students focus on important words and would help them self-monitor for meaning.

\# *   *So You Want to be President* by Judith St.George, New York: Philomel Books, 2000.
This book about our first 41 presidents is a great model of good writing; it comes alive with small, interesting details that support a few main ideas.

(P)   *Who Hops?* By Katie Davis, New York: Harcourt, Inc., 1998.
This book uses very simple text and big, bold illustrations to present some basic animal facts. It encourages children to listen for information that doesn't make sense.

\# *   *Will We Miss Them? Endangered Species* by Alexandra Wright, Watertown (MA): Charlesbridge Publishing, 1992.
This beautiful picture book (by an 11-year-old girl) describes the natural environment and the plight of many different endangered species. A simple, direct presentation.

Texts for Use in Blended Strategy Practice and Guided Strategy Applications

Anthologies of Short Stories

It's not easy finding anthologies of short stories suitable for elementary grade readers, but these sources fit the bill nicely. The stories in these books vary in length from just a couple of pages to about ten pages. Purchasing a few copies of different anthologies will provide several weeks' worth of reading for your students during their small group instruction.

Birthday Surprises by Johanna Hurwitz (Ed.), New York: Morrow Junior Books, 1995.
Editor Hurwitz sent the same prompt to several children's authors: You receive a beautifully wrapped birthday gift in the mail and open it up. There is nothing inside. Use this idea as a launching point for your story. Responses to this prompt were compiled into this delightful multi-genre book containing stories and poems from many of the authors students know and love.

Dog to the Rescue by Jeannette Sanderson, New York: Scholastic, 1993.
Seventeen tales of dog heroism are contained in this book, written at about a fourth-grade reading level.

Every Living Thing by Cynthia Rylant, New York: Simon and Schuster, 1985.
My all-time-favorite anthology of short stories is this thin volume, which contains 12 stories, all featuring animals in a central way. Stories vary a bit in level of sophistication.

Five True Dog Stories by Margaret Davidson, New York: Scholastic, 1977.
These engaging stories look like garden-variety, middle-level text, but they're actually written at a second grade reading level. In this same series you can also find the following: *True Dolphin Stories, True Cat Stories, True Horse Stories.*

Front Porch Stories at the One Room School by Eleanor Tate, New York: Dell Books, 1992.
These 10 short, down-home tales of African-American life in the South give readers a glimpse of this culture and community. Well written text at about a fourth-grade reading level.

Girls Who Rocked the World: Heroines from Sacagawea to Sheryl Swoopes by Amelie Welden, New York: Scholastic, 1998.
This volume tells the stories of 33 girls, past and present, who changed history before reaching their twenties. Each biography contains a photo of its subject as well as photos and quotes by young girls today with dreams of rocking the world in their own way.

It's Fine to be Nine: *Stories about Being Nine*, Scholastic, 1998.
>This volume contains stand-alone chapters from many of the chapter books known and loved by children approximately nine years old. For example, there are chapters from *Ramona Forever* (Cleary), *Tales of a Fourth Grade Nothing* (Blume), and *Fourth Grade Rats* (Spinelli). In this same series, you can also find the following titles: *It's Heaven to Be Seven* and *It's Great to Be Eight.*

Native American Stories told by Joseph Bruchac, Golden, (CO): Fulcrum Publishing, 1991.
>This collection of myths drawn from the native cultures of North America depicts the native view of the world as family. This volume contains stories from a variety of native American traditions.

New Kids in Town: Oral Histories of Immigrant Teens by Janet Bode, New York: Scholastic, 1989.
>Eleven teen immigrants tell their courageous stories of coming to America from various corners of the world.

The People Could Fly: American Black Folktales told by Virginia Hamilton, New York: Alfred A. Knopf, 1985.
>This anthology (also perfect for storytelling) contains animal tales, tales of the fanciful and supernatural, and tales of freedom. Dramatic illusrations, too!

Ribbiting Tales edited by Nancy Springer, New York: Puffin Books, 2000.
>The eight stories in this book are all about frogs—by many authors that children know including Bruce Coville, Brian Jacques, and Jane Yolen.

Scary Stories to Tell in the Dark retold by Alvin Schwartz, New York: Harper and Row Publishers, 1991.
>Kids love these tales about eerie horror and dark revenge, but before you use this material as part of your reading curriculum, it would be wise to check with your administrator and parents. Also in this series you will find, *More Scary Stories to Tell in the Dark.*

The Stone Soup Book of Friendship Stories: The Best of Stone Soup, the Magazine by Young Writers edited by William Rubel and Gerry Mandel, New York: Scholastic, 1998.
>The 22 stories in this book depict dimensions of friendship deemed important to the young authors who wrote them. The stories are appropriate for students ages eight through thirteen.

Stories to Solve: Folktales from Around the World told by George Shannon, New York: Scholastic, 1985.
>Each of these *very* short folktales is a puzzle to be solved through cleverness, common sense, or close attention to details in the text. The book offers a great opportunity for older readers to apply critical thinking skills!

The Tales of Uncle Remus: The Adventures of Brer Rabbit told by Julius Lester, New York: Penguin Books, 1987.
>Lester's retelling of these timeless tales keeps alive a cultural tradition that is all but unknown to today's generation of children. Brer Rabbit's spunk and vigor in these 48 short tales set a worthy (and often humorous) example for young readers.

Ten True Animal Rescues by Jeanne Betancourt, New York: Scholastic, 1998.
>Ten true stories about animals who saved the lives of their owners or complete strangers. Third-grade reading level.

A Terrifying Taste of Short and Shivery: Thirty Creepy Tales told by Robert San Souci, New York: Delacorte Press, 1998.
>Horrific stories such as these sometimes motivate our most reluctant readers, when other literature has failed to entice them. Again, checking with parents and administrators before you use this book in your classroom may save you distress later on.

They Led the Way: 14 American Women by Johanna Johnston, New York: Scholastic, 1973.
>The stories of these women are proof that the world has many places and possibilities for women as well as for men. (I'm always looking for books that represent a "strong girl" theme, and this one is perfect!)

Thimbleberry Stories by Cynthia Rylant, New York: Harcourt, Inc, 2000.
>The endearing animal characters in this book will remind you of the characters you remember from the Thornton Burgess books of a bygone era. There are four sweet stories in this book, all beautifully crafted.

Two-Minute Mysteries by Donald J. Sobol, New York: Scholastic, 1967.
>This book by the same author as the *Encyclopedia Brown* series contains more than 50 one-page mysteries for students to solve. Great opportunities for noticing and synthesizing small details.

Books of Poetry
Many of the poets included below have written other books, as well. The books listed here happen to be the ones that are on my shelves at home.

Multiple Volumes by Favorite Poets of Children and Adolescents
When children find a poet they enjoy, they seek other books by that same author. Shel Silverstein is a perfect example! *Where the Sidewalk Ends* was so popular in my classroom during my early years of teaching that I purchased several copies to try to keep up with the demand. Fortunately, Mr. Silverstein cooperated by writing some other poetry books, as well. And a lot of other poets have also produced more than one anthology of their works. A few of my favorites are listed here.

Mr. Silverstein may have done more than any other modern poet to turn poetry into a genre-of-choice for children. His mysterious charms, demonstrated in these three volumes, will likely captivate even the most reluctant reader. The only downside to the Silverstein phenomenon is that today's children now expect *all* poetry to follow in the tradition of this poet's zany wit and masterful capacity to play with words.

>*Where the Sidewalk Ends* by Shel Silverstein, New York: Harper Collins, 1974.

>*A Light in the Attic* by Shel Silverstein, New York: Harper Collins, 1981.

>*Falling Up* by Shel Silverstein, New York: Harper Collins, 1996.

Jack Prelutsky crafts poetry that immediately wins the hearts of young readers. Maybe it's his choice of subjects close to children's own experiences. Maybe it's his humor, built upon outrageous exaggeration. Maybe it's the uncanny surprise endings to many of his poems. It's hard not to laugh out loud when you're reading poetry by Jack Prelutsky.

>*The New Kid on the Block* by Jack Prelutsky, New York: Scholastic, 1984.

>*Something Big Has Been Here* by Jack Prelutsky, New York: Green Willow Books, 1990.

>*A Pizza the Size of the Sun* by Jack Prelutsky, New York: Scholastic, 1994.

As I travel around doing workshops, I've discovered that many teachers are unfamiliar with Sara Holbrook, and that is unfortunate. What she writes, whether about topics that are light and humorous or topics that are deeply moving, speaks to adolescents in a way that is passionate and personal. She captures the spirit of those turbulent teen years with a sensitivity that middle-school and high-school teachers will welcome in their classrooms.

> *Nothing's the End of the World* by Sara Holbrook, Honesdale, PA: Boyds Mills Press, 1995.

> *Am I Naturally this Crazy?* By Sara Holbrook, Honesdale, PA: Boyds Mills Press, 1996.

> *Walking on the Boundaries of Change* by Sara Holbrook, Honesdale, PA: Boyds Mills Press, 1998.

> *I Never Said I Wasn't Difficult* by Sara Holbrook, Honesdale, PA: Boyds Mills Press, 1996.

> *The Dog Ate My Homework* by Sara Holbrook, Honesdale, PA: Boyds Mills Press, 1996.

Bruce Lansky has edited several small volumes of humorous poems around themes like "school," "friends," and "disasters." Lots of the poets children know and love are represented in these anthologies, like John Ciardi, Judith Viorst, Ogden Nash, and Douglas Florian.

> *Kids Pick the Funniest Poems* edited by Bruce Lansky, New York: Meadowbrook Press, 1991.

> *Miles of Smiles* edited by Bruce Lansky, New York: Meadowbrook Press, 1998.

> *A Bad Case of the Giggles* edited by Bruce Lansky, New York: Meadowbrook Press, 1994.

Poems Written around a Particular Topic or Theme

A poet's voice can bring a powerful perspective to a particular topic or theme. So keep poetry in mind as you search for reading materials to support a social studies or science unit. Poetry is also an excellent way for students to examine a different culture in greater depth.

> *Bird Watch* by Jane Yolen, New York: Penguin Putnam Books, 1990.
> A great resource for science class, as well as for literature study, this book brings nature, poetry, and art together in 17 beautiful poems about birds. They soar off the page!

> *A Chill in the Air: Nature Poems for Fall and Winter* by John Frank, New York: Simon and Schuster, 2003.
> The short poems in this beautifully illustrated book depict images of winter from the last falling leaves to the first buds on springtime branches. A delight for lovers of language, regardless of age.

> *Dear Mother, Dear Daughter* by Jane Yolen and Heidi E. Y. Stemple, Honesdale, PA: Boyds Mills Press, 2001.
> The poems in this little volume by Jane Yolen and her daughter are written as a series of letters from mother to daughter and from daughter to mother around topics that are perennial favorites in a parent-child relationship: cleaning your bedroom, doing homework, talking on the phone, etc. These poems are excellent for teaching point-of-view in a piece of literature.

Subjects that seem to work well in modeling sessions often involve real kids solving real problems.

The Flag of Childhood: Poems from the Middle East selected by Naomi Shihab Nye, New York: Aladdin Paperbacks, 1998.
This anthology of 60 poems from Palestine, Israel, Egypt, Iraq, and elsewhere in the Middle East provides a glimpse into the hearts and minds of people we know mostly through a veil of stereotypes. Between the lines of these poems we find that our human connections are more powerful than our cultural differences. Many of these poems are most suitable for older readers.

Hailstones and Halibut Bones by Mary O'Neill, New York: Doubleday, 1989.
I remember using this book of poems about different colors during my first year of teaching, and I'm still using it today. In new editions, illustrations have been redone, adding even more liveliness to this favorite classic.

If You're Not Here, Please Raise Your Hand by Kalli Dakos, New York: Simon and Schuster, 1990.
Your students will find a lot they can relate to in this little book of poems about school.

In Daddy's Arms I am Tall: African Americans Celebrating Fathers illustrated by Javaka Steptoe, New York: Lee and Low Books, 1990.
Several African-American poets contribute their voices to this richly illustrated book that celebrates the role of fathers in the African-American experience. Best for older readers.

Lemonade Sun and Other Summer Poems by Rebecca Kai Dotlich Honesdale, PA: Boyds Mills Press, 1998.
These charming poems, accompanied by equally charming illustrations, bring to life the sights and sounds of summer in any season of the year. A treat for all ages.

Make a Joyful Sound: Poems for Children by African-American Poets edited by Deborah Slier, New York: Scholastic, 1991.
While many of the poems in this book celebrate the history, dreams, and achievements of African-Americans, *all* children will be touched by the strength, beauty, and love that these poems represent.

Meet Danitra Brown by Nikki Grimes, New York: Scholastic, 1984.
This is a splendiferous collection of poems all about a splendiferous little African- American girl, Danitra Brown.

Silver Seeds by Paul Paolilli and Dan Brewer, New York: Penguin Books, 2001.
A description of this book cannot adequately convey its effectiveness. Its simple acrostics and spectacular illustrations treat readers to a new view of icons of the natural world, which we see every day, but do not usually look at closely enough.

Soul Looks Back in Wonder illustrated by Tom Feelings, New York: Puffin Books, 1993.
The spirit of African creativity comes to life in this dazzling collection of pictures and poems by authors including Maya Angelou, Walter Dean Myers, and Langston Hughes. Best for older readers.

(P) *You Read to Me, I'll Read to You: Very Short Stories to Read Together* by Mary Ann Hoberman, New York: Little, Brown and Company, 2001.
These lively poems, perfect for young children, are written in two voices, all concluding in a love for reading, "You read to me, I'll read to you."

Don't Forget about Poetry Classics

Call me old-fashioned, but no child should grow up without experiencing the magical words of poetry greats, such as Robert Louis Stevenson, A. A. Milne, and Emily Dickinson (to name just a few). Share your special childhood favorites with the children in your class. These classics will stretch your students' thinking and give them plenty of opportunities to use all of their comprehension strategies as they construct meaning from these timeless texts.

> *Every Time I Climb a Tree* by David McCord, New York: Little, Brown and Company, 1967.
> David McCord takes ordinary things like fences, jam, and rocks, and creates word-magic on the page with language and rhythm that make ideas dance into the reader's heart.

> *I'm Nobody! Who Are You? Poems of Emily Dickinson for Children,* Owings Mills, MD: Stemmer House, 1978.
> I've had success using several of these poems with children in the fifth and sixth grades.

> *Knock at a Star: A Child's Introduction to Poetry* edited by X.J. Kennedy and Dorothy M. Kennedy, New York: Little, Brown and Company, 1999.
> This volume discusses with readers what poems can do, what's inside a poem, and different kinds of poetry. In addition to including many wonderful poems that carry us back to the poetry we may have enjoyed in our own childhood, these editors help young writers understand what's involved in making poetry come alive.

(P)　*Read-aloud Rhymes for the Very Young* selected by Jack Prelutsky, New York: Alfred A. Knopf, 1986.
> More than 200 (mostly very short) poems about topics and themes relevant to early childhood are accompanied by whimsical illustrations, offering young learners a fanciful introduction to language that rhymes.

> *A Swinger of Birches*: *Poems of Robert Frost for Young People* edited by Barbara Holdridge, Owings Mills, MD: Stemmer House.
> Although the poetry of Robert Frost is somewhat advanced for elementary grade children, active use of comprehension strategies will help children access its meaning. And the vibrant illustrations in this book will surely contribute to readers' enjoyment and the richness of these beautiful poems.

This book does not contain any bibliography of longer texts suitable for independent-reading assignments. The possibilities for such assignments are so vast it would be nearly impossible to compile a list that in any way represents even a small sampling of the best books appropriate for any grade level. As you select chapter books for your students to read independently, think about a theme and other characteristics that appeal to children the age of the students you teach. Try to expose your young readers to a variety of genres and a variety of authors. And always, always consider their reading level. Remember that books that students read independently should be easier than those through which you teach reading. Students should be able to decode and understand their independent reading books with ease.

Strategy Mini-Posters, Cue Cards, and Bookmarks

CONNECTING

Finding something that is connected:

- To my life
- To another book
- To things in the world

PICTURING

If I close my eyes,

- I can see. . . . .

- I can hear. . . . .

- I can feel. . . . .

- I can smell. . . . .

- I can taste. . . . .

WONDERING

What questions pop into my mind, such as:

- What might happen next?
- How will [the story] end?
- Why did the author write this?
- What else do I want to know?

GUESSING
(PREDICTING)

- What might happen next?
- How will [the story] end?
- What is the author trying to tell me?

NOTICING

- What are the important clues?
- Have I guessed right or wrong?
- Is there something I don't understand?
- Has the author done something crafty?

FIGURING OUT

- How do all the clues fit together?

- When did that "little light bulb" go on in my head?

- What do I understand better after this reading?

CONNECTING

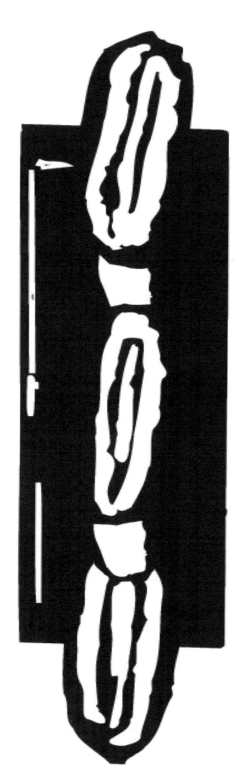

PICTURING

WONDERING

GUESSING

NOTICING

FIGURING OUT

METACOGNITION

(met-a-cog-ni-tion)

means

Thinking about Thinking

GUESSING/ PREDICTING

What will I *probably* learn from this text?

CONNECTING

What do I already know about this topic?

WONDERING

What questions will this text probably answer?

Who—What—When—Where—Why—How

PICTURING

What clues in the illustrations can help me to understand this reading?

NOTICING

What clues do I notice in this text that can help me to understand it?

FIGURING OUT

Do I have a plan for figuring out the big ideas and the supporting evidence?

Connecting

Guessing

Picturing

Noticing

Wondering

Figuring Out

Name:	Name.	Name.
Connecting 	**Connecting** 	**Connecting** 
Picturing	**Picturing**	**Picturing**
Wondering	**Wondering** 	**Wondering** 
Guessing 	**Guessing** 	**Guessing** 
Noticing 	**Noticing** 	**Noticing** 
Figuring Out 	**Figuring Out** 	**Figuring Out** 

GROWING PROFESSIONALLY THROUGH THE STUDY OF COMPREHENSION

Reflecting on the Teaching of Comprehension: Some Questions for Study Groups

Introduction: A New View of Comprehension Strategy Instruction

1. What frustrations do you face in the teaching of comprehension?

2. If you asked your students to describe what they do in your classroom for "reading comprehension," what would they say?

3. Has comprehension instruction in your classroom changed within the past few years? If it has, in what way(s) has it changed?

4. What questions do you have about the teaching of comprehension?

Chapter One: Helping Children Think about Thinking: Introducing Reading Comprehension Strategies Using Kid-Friendly Language

1. Do you think it would be helpful to students at the grade level you teach to use the kid-friendly strategy labels? Why? Why not?

2. Have you ever thought about introducing strategies together, rather than one at a time? Do you think this method of introducing the strategies makes sense? Why? Why not?

3. Do you think the kind of strategy introduction described in this chapter would work in your classroom? If not, what kind of modifications might be appropriate?

4. As you introduce comprehension strategies to your students, reflect on what goes well and what doesn't go well. What might you do differently during a similar explanation next time?

Chapter Two: Thinking Out Loud: Modeling Reading Comprehension Strategies

1. How much instructional time do you typically devote to modeling?

2. Are your students focused and attentive when you model? If not, what could you do differently to maintain their attention?

3. What do you consider to be the key components of successful modeling?

4. Have you used any short texts for modeling that you would recommend to other teachers at your grade level?

Chapter Three: Guided Student Practice:
Using Comprehension Strategies in a Small Group

1. Practicing the use of comprehension strategies in this integrated, interactive manner probably means that students will not read extensive amounts of text during small group instruction. How can you make sure that students are also reading longer text during the school day?

2. Although students are active meaning makers within this practice model, the activity is more teacher-directed than, for example, literature circles, where students construct meaning without the teacher present. What other kinds of literacy opportunities can you create in your classroom so that students may apply comprehension strategies collaboratively, with their peers?

3. What problems do you foresee in the implementation of this practice model in your classroom? How could you deal with these problems proactively?

4. Working with small groups of students presents problems with management in some classrooms. From your experiences as a teacher, what have you learned about classroom management that could help other teachers address the same dilemma?

5. Short text for practicing comprehension strategies is sometimes difficult to find. Where could you acquire suitable materials for your grade level? (Don't forget about those old basals that are gathering dust in the back of some closet at your school.)

6. How might this practice model look at the primary grade level? The intermediate grade level? The middle-school level?

Chapter Four: Getting Past Mediocre Strategy Instruction

1. If you could offer only *one* piece of advice to the teacher in this classroom, what would you say? Why do you consider this the most critical suggestion to make at this time?

2. Think about the lesson described in this chapter: What are some of the features of this lesson that you would like to apply to your classroom? What features of this lesson would you like to avoid?

3. Could you and a colleague become each other's "critical friend" and use the questions suggested here for analyzing a lesson in the use of comprehension strategies? How could you set this up?

Chapter Five: Applying Reading Comprehension Strategies
to Study Fiction

1. Intensive strategy instruction usually means a focus on a broadly defined comprehension strategy: *connecting, picturing,* etc. Do you think more specifically focused instruction would benefit students? Why? Why not?

2. Which of these possible strategy applications would be useful to you at your grade level?

3. What author, theme, and genre studies would you like to incorporate into your literacy curriculum?

4. What other suggestions for author, theme, and genre studies would work well at your grade level?

Chapter Six: Applying Comprehension Strategies in the Content Areas

1. Although we know we should be using informational text to teach reading, we typically teach reading with narrative fiction. Why do you think we don't use informational text more often?

2. Do you have some students in your class who prefer to read informational text? How do you accommodate their interests?

3. What do you consider some of the important differences between teaching comprehension strategies within fiction and teaching comprehension strategies within informational text?

4. How do you handle the problem of below-level readers confronted by informational text that is too difficult for them?

5. What informational texts have been particularly popular with students at the grade level you teach?

Chapter Seven: Teaching Comprehension Strategies in Shared, Guided, Independent Reading

1. Do you provide an appropriate balance among shared, guided, and independent reading in your classroom? Do you rely on one of these ways of "doing reading" more than others?

2. In which area do you think you do the best job teaching: shared, guided, or independent reading? What makes you think this?

3. What factors make it difficult for you as a teacher of shared reading? Guided reading? Independent reading?

4. What do you consider the next step for you in becoming an even better teacher of shared reading? Guided reading? Independent reading?

Chapter Eight: Assessing Students' Reading Comprehension and Comprehension Strategy Use

1. Has focusing on comprehension strategies in your classroom improved your students' comprehension of what they read? What evidence supports your answer?

2. What problems with the use of comprehension strategies do your students seem to experience? How have you addressed these problems?

3. How do you monitor students' comprehension? What means of monitoring your students' reading comprehension works best for you in your classroom?

4. How well do your students respond in writing to open-ended comprehension questions? To what do you attribute their success or lack of success?

If you could offer one piece of advice to the teacher in this classroom, what would you say?

Bibliography of Professional Resources

Many researchers and educators have written about comprehension instruction. And I am grateful for the insights that they have shared. It is because of the scholars and educators who have preceded me in the study of comprehension and in the teaching of comprehension that I was able to imagine and implement *my* vision of comprehension instruction. Below is an annotated list of some of the resources that guided my journey as an educator and as a scholar of education. As you will see, I've divided this bibliography among several different areas of interest.

Digging Deeper into Comprehension Research and Instruction

National Reading Panel (2000). *Teaching children to read: An evidence-based assessment of the scientific research literature on reading and its implications for reading instruction.* Bethesda, MD: National Institute of Child Health and Human Development.
The National Reading Panel has identified several comprehension strategies in addition to the repertoire of metacognitive strategies described here. There is some controversy over this panel's report in part due to this panel's definition of what counts as research and questions over the reliability of their conclusions. (Many of the studies used were very small, and so the statistical significance of the studies was negligible.) However, this report represents a considerable effort to synthesize an extensive body of research findings, and it is certainly worth perusing. There is a brief *Summary*, about 34 pages, with three pages from this summary devoted to the area of comprehension. The full report contains the *Reports of the Subgroups*, with over 130 pages related to comprehension, and there are plenty of useful appendices.

Block, C. & Pressley, M. (Eds.) (2002). *Comprehension instruction: Research-based best practices.* New York: Guilford Press.
This book isn't light reading, so don't bother taking it along to the beach. However, it is well worth the time and effort needed to digest its contents. Cathy Collins Block and Michael Pressley have compiled chapters by many educators who are well known and respected for their research in the area of comprehension. One of my favorite chapters is the first in the book, written by Michael Pressley: *Comprehension Strategies Instruction: A Turn-of-the-Century Status Report.* In this chapter, he identifies current teaching practices related to comprehension and discusses how they measure up against research findings. The book is divided into three main sections, with chapters focused on "Theoretical Foundations", "Branching Out and Expanding Our Horizons in the 21st Century", and "Comprehension Instruction in Preschool, Primary, and Intermediate Grades."

Duffy, G. (2003). *Explaining reading: A resource for teaching concepts, skills, and strategies.* New York: Guilford Press.
    This little book is remarkably explicit about the nature of explicit instruction. For each of the comprehension strategies, it outlines in chart-form: how you will know when you need to teach the strategy, conceptual understandings that students must have in place, the student's objective, and hints for using the strategy effectively. It even tells you how to introduce, model, and scaffold the strategy. In addition to helping teachers explain comprehension strategies, this book also supports explicit instruction in the areas of vocabulary, word recognition, and fluency.

Pearson, P.D. and Gallagher, M.C. (1983). "The Instruction of Reading Comprehension." *Contemporary Educational Psychology.* 8: 317-344.
    In this journal article, Pearson and Gallagher explain the gradual release of responsibility in the explicit teaching of comprehension. They also show graphically, through a chart, the reciprocal nature of teacher/learner roles as instruction moves from its initial phase with the teacher in charge of the learning task, to the final instructional phase where students are entirely independent in their application of the new learning. The information in this article has guided both scholars and practitioners as they strive to improve comprehension instruction.

Pressley, M., El-Dinary, P.B., Gaskins, I., Schuder, T., Bergman, J.L., Almasi, J., &Brown, R. (1992). "Beyond direct explanation: Transactional instruction of reading comprehension strategies." *Elementary School Journal*, 92: 511-554.
    This is just one of the articles authored by Pressley and a number of his colleagues that provides research validation for teaching a repertoire of comprehension strategies, rather than teaching one strategy at a time. My "Kid-Friendly" approach was guided extensively by this belief that the best comprehension instruction is *transactional*: There are transactions between group members. There are transactions between reader and text. And there are transactions within a social context whereby the interpretation of text derived by a group of students and a teacher working together is different from the meaning that any one reader would have created alone. A thorough description of Transactional Strategy Instruction may also be found in *Comprehension instruction: Research-based best practices* (cited above), in the chapter, "Challenges of Implementing Transactional Strategies Instruction for Reading Comprehension," by Pamela Beard El-Dinary.

Digging Deeper into the Explicit Teaching of Individual Comprehension Strategies (Books)

Harvey, S. & Goudvis, A. (2000). *Strategies that work: Teaching comprehension to enhance understanding.* York, ME: Stenhouse.
    This book is an excellent companion to *Mosaic of Thought*; it addresses the same seven strategies (although, also, one-at-a-time). But this text is more of a classroom resource, containing a variety of clearly presented lessons for teaching the individual strategies. And the valuable appendices include several bibliographies for comprehension strategy teaching.

Keene, E. & Zimmermann, S. (1997). *Mosaic of thought: Teaching comprehension in a reader's workshop.* Portsmouth, NH: Heinemann.

This book identifies seven research-based comprehension strategies and describes classroom scenarios from various grades in which these strategies are taught explicitly. Although I am not in agreement with Keene and Zimmermann's practice of "teaching one strategy at a time over several weeks," this book provides a good foundation for teachers who want to acquaint themselves with the look and feel of classrooms where comprehension strategies are taught explicitly. The book is more a source of motivation and less a "how to" guide. And it is a wonderful book for a professional study group, where teachers can talk together about points that intrigue them.

Miller, D. (2002). *Reading with meaning: Teaching comprehension in the primary grades.* Portland, ME: Stenhouse.

This book answers a lot of questions about what teaching individual comprehension strategies looks like in the early primary grades. The author, Debbie Miller, who was a first-grade teacher for many years, shares her expertise, as well as her passion for teaching reading. Four pages in the middle of the book are filled with photographs of her classroom, a testimony to the value of a rich literacy environment. Her book maintains a conversational tone throughout.

Digging Deeper into Issues Related to Struggling Readers

Allington, Richard. (2001). *What really matters for struggling readers: Designing research based programs.* New York: Longman.

Contained within the pages of this thin volume with a great deal of author-voice are research-based answers to the question, "What really matters for struggling readers?" Allington identifies four critical points: Kids need to read a lot; Kids need books they can read; Kids need to learn to read fluently; Kids need to develop thoughtful literacy.

The author concludes the book with a chapter on "Improving Classroom Instruction," in which he reminds teachers that "the most powerful feature of schools, in terms of developing children as readers and writers, is the quality of classroom instruction." He then tries to define dimensions of this instructional quality. The chapter also contains a useful model for reflecting on professional literature in a professional study group (TAPER).

Digging Deeper into the Assessment of Comprehension Strategy Use

Schmidt, M. C. (1990). *"A questionnaire to measure children's awareness of strategic reading processes." The Reading Teacher.* 43(7), 454-461.

This article contains a "Metacomprehension Strategy Index," in which students are directed to select a multiple-choice response to 25 questions about what good readers do before, during, and after reading. Although *knowing* what to do and actually *doing* the right thing are not always synonymous, using this instrument can be a useful first step in evaluating students' use of comprehension strategies: First, is there a mismatch between what the reader states and what good readers do and what the teacher observes the child doing to enhance comprehension? Second, does the child realize what good readers should do during each phase of the reading process? If a survey such as this tells us that a student is unclear about the behaviors of good readers, we shouldn't be too surprised when that student displays few good reader behaviors.

Digging Deeper into Text Selection

Horning, K.T.,(1997). *From cover to cover: Evaluating and reviewing children's books.* New York: Harper Collins.
    This very practical book explains what to look for and how to evaluate several different types of children's books including the following: books of information, traditional literature such as myths, legends, tall tales, and folk tales, poetry, picture books, easy readers and transitional books, and fiction. I've used many of the ideas in this book to help students understand the characteristics of different types of text.

Syzmusiak, K., & Sibberson, F. (2001). *Beyond leveled books: Supporting transitional readers in grades 2-5.* Portland, ME: Stenhouse.
    This excellent book describes the needs of "transitional readers" (students ready for easy chapter books, but not quite capable of tackling more advanced, "Newbery quality" literature). This book also defines the qualities of good transitional level texts. Choosing "just right" books is difficult for students in the intermediate grades. And the information in this book can make that task much more manageable.

Digging Deeper into Comprehension of Informational Texts

Hoyt, L, Mooney, M., & Parkes, B. (2003). *Exploring informational texts: From theory to practice.* Portsmouth, NH: Heinemann.
    This very readable book includes insights into features of informational texts that are the most critical to teach, the use of informational text within primary-level guided reading, as well as instruction in math and other subjects. And this book links guided reading of informational text with guided writing. This book is especially appropriate for teachers of primary-grade students. It includes sample mini-lessons that would work well with young readers.

Moss, B. (2003). *Exploring the literature of fact: Children's nonfiction trade books in the elementary classroom.* New York: Guilford.
    Easily one of the best books I've read about the use of informational text in the classroom. Although the focus is *trade books* rather than *text books,* the bibliographies in every chapter (all annotated!) can make it easy to locate other forms of informational text matched to any content study. Among the many topics covered are suggested guidelines for book selection, hints for reading nonfiction aloud, and many instructional techniques for getting kids to respond to nonfiction text. There's help here for teachers from the early grades right through middle school.

The scholars who preceded me in the study of comprehension made it possible for me to imagine and implement my vision of comprehension instruction.

List of Files Included on CD

(*) denotes that a Spanish translation is available in the Spanish_Translation folder.